The Challenge of Law Reform

The Challenge

of Law Reform

BY ARTHUR T. VANDERBILT

Chief Justice, Supreme Court of New Jersey

Princeton University Press

Princeton, New Jersey

1955

Preface

LAST YEAR when Dean Ribble of the University of Virginia Law School invited me to deliver the William H. White Lectures (named in honor of a distinguished alumnus who was for many years a member of its Board of Visitors), I decided to take as my subject the matter which has most concerned me in my work on the bench —the improvement of the administration of justice in the courts. In these unsettled days when every good citizen should be giving thought to how to best preserve individual freedom while at the same time strengthening the processes of government, it seems to me that the solution of the problems of improving the caliber of judges, jurors, and lawyers, of eliminating technicalities and surprise in trials, and of installing sound business methods in the judicial system has an immediacy that the bench, the bar, and the law schools generally have failed to recognize but of which the public, especially litigants, are all too well aware.

I realize, of course, that these troublesome problems can never be solved ideally—perfect justice is obviously seldom attainable in a workaday world—but I do know from experience that the solution of these problems may be approximated if there is the will to do so on the part of the legal profession, or on the part of the public if the bar defaults on its obligation. The practical solution of these problems, given a real determination to do so, is much simpler than most people suspect. It is not knowledge of ways and means that we lack in most instances; it is the will to put them into effect.

Because at the time I could speak of the proposed bill for a Judicial Conference in New York State only in a tentative way, Dean Ribble has accorded me permission to revise that portion of my lectures in the light of the enactment of the bill into law.

All of the matters that I have dealt with for improving the administration of justice are necessary preliminaries to the undertaking of what seems to me to be the great task of the law in the second half of the twentieth century, the simplification and modernization of the corpus of our substantive law to bring it in line with the needs of the times. The most cursory examination of our substantive law as a system will reveal the need for such a project. I envision it as the greatest task that remains to be undertaken in the history of Anglo-American jurisprudence. I had merely time to mention it in my lectures, but Dean Ribble has authorized me to expand my views on the subject in a concluding chapter.

To Dean Ribble and his faculty and the student body of the Law School I am much indebted for a very responsive audience and for a week of delightful hospitality in the Blue Ridge Mountains that I shall long remember.

ARTHUR T. VANDERBILT

Newark, New Jersey
May 9, 1955

Contents

PREFACE v

  I. THE NEED FOR REFORM 3

 II. BETTER JUDGES AND BETTER JURORS ... 11

III. SIMPLIFIED JUDICIAL STRUCTURE
        AND PROCEDURE 36

IV. EFFECTIVE ADMINISTRATION
        AND LESS DELAY 76

 V. MODERNIZING THE LAW
        THROUGH LAW CENTERS 134

INDEX 185

The Challenge of Law Reform

CHAPTER I

The Need for Reform

"JUSTICE," said Daniel Webster in his eulogy of Mr. Justice Story, "is the great interest of man on earth." [1] Much as we wish this were so, there is unfortunately a staggering mass of evidence to the contrary.

Major crimes in the United States reached an all time high in 1954, exceeding the two million mark for the third successive year. [2] In spite of the publicity given the famous Kefauver Committee, Congress failed to implement its program against the political allies of organized crime, although local conditions were improved. Another great danger to the Republic is the apathy of its citizens; only sixty-one per cent of the eligible voters bothered to exercise their franchise in the presidential election of 1952, in spite of the attention which all the mass media of communication focused on the contest. Can citizens who will not even take the trouble to vote for a president every four years be expected to be interested in justice?

But there are others, besides the average citizen, who have a more intimate duty to be concerned about jus-

---

[1] William Story, ed., *Life and Letters of Joseph Story*, 622, 624 (1851).

[2] Federal Bureau of Investigation, *Uniform Crime Reports for the United States, 1954*, Vol. XXV, No. 2, p. 69.

tice. I speak of judges and lawyers. I am convinced that
the criminals, the gangsters, the corrupt local officials,
the communistic subversives, and the apathetic citizens
are no more dangerous to their communities and to the
country at large than the judges, many of them amiable
gentlemen, who oppose either openly or covertly every
change in procedural law and administration that would
serve to eliminate technicalities, surprise, and undue delay in the law simply because they would be called upon
to learn new rules of procedure or new and more effective methods of work. Their number is legion. I must
bracket with them the multitude of lawyers who, although they know the defects of the law from personal
experience as well as from the complaints of their
clients, likewise oppose all reform, either for the same
selfish reasons as the judges or, worse yet, out of supine
subservience to them. Whenever I come upon a judge
or a lawyer who insists that improvement in judicial
administration is impossible of attainment because, as
he puts it, "Things are different in my state," I know I
am dealing with a man who is more dangerous to the
country than the criminals, the communistic subversives
and the host of indifferent citizens, because he gives the
public the impression that he believes all is well in the
house of the law, although many litigants find plenty
of just causes for dissatisfaction. It is in the courts and
not in the legislature that our citizens primarily feel the
keen, cutting edge of the law. If they have respect for
the work of the courts, their respect for law will survive
the shortcomings of every other branch of government;

but if they lose their respect for the work of the courts, their respect for law and order will vanish with it to the great detriment of society, for it surely does not have to be argued that respect for law is all important for the survival of popular government. A decision based on technicalities or surprise, or a trial or a decision unduly delayed, or even a case of judicial bad manners can kill respect for law more disastrously than any disagreement on some abstruse question of substantive law.

Is it not commercialism that causes many of our lawyers to oppose reform, a commercialism that manifests itself in a preoccupation with private law and a neglect of public law and government? Two of our great Chief Justices have expressed this far more bluntly than I should dare to do. Over thirty years ago Chief Justice Taft complained, "The whole tendency of the last twenty-five years in the profession, as in all society, has been toward commercialism." And in 1934 Chief Justice Stone asserted: [3]

"Commercialism has made the learned profession of an earlier day the obsequious servant of business and tainted it with the morals and manners of the marketplace in its more anti-social manifestations. Candor would compel even those of us who have the most abiding faith in our profession to admit that in our time the Bar has not maintained its traditional posi-

[3] Taft, "Legal Ethics," 1 *Boston University Law Rev.* 233, at 244 (1921). Cf. Stone, *Dedicatory Exercises of the Law Quadrangle,* University of Michigan Law School, p. 47 (1934).

tion of public influence and leadership. . . . More and more the lawyer looks for his reward to the material benefits that too often tend to obscure his larger vision; that sometimes weaken even the confidence of clients in the lawyer's devotion to his interests."

There was a time when it was deemed sacrilegious to question the conduct of a judge or to doubt the fiction that had come down through the centuries that the law, especially the unwritten law, was the perfection of reason. In 1906 Roscoe Pound, then a young lawyer from Nebraska, ventured to address the American Bar Association meeting in St. Paul on "The Causes of Popular Dissatisfaction with the Administration of Justice." [4] Notwithstanding the fact that his presentation was factual, fully documented, and quite unemotional, the leaders of the bar of that day were so aghast at the questioning of what "the wisdom of the centuries had built up," to quote one of these anguished souls, that they defeated a resolution for the immediate printing of 4,000 copies of the speech. Years later Dean Wigmore referred to the speech as "the spark that kindled the white flame of progress." [5] The intervening half century has witnessed a great change in our attitude toward the inadequacies of the law and of its servants. Perhaps the upsurge of science is teaching us to face facts as they are. Inescapably every serious student of the law is aware of the necessity for adapting the substantive law

[4] 29 A.B.A. Rep. 395 (Part I, 1906).
[5] 20 *J. Am. Jud. Soc.* 176 (1937).

to the needs of the times, a stupendous task that cannot be indefinitely postponed. But not so many are aware of the mood of the public toward the courts, the law, and lawyers, and they do not realize that there are problems of personnel and procedure that must be given precedence over the improvement of the substantive law. These problems must be speedily resolved if we are to safeguard the judicial system by making it responsive to the reasonable demands of the times. Ours is a rapidly changing civilization and the courts cannot hope to decide today's controversies adequately with the outmoded procedure of bygone centuries.

Fortunately, despite the opposition of backward-looking judges and lawyers, among some groups of lawyers there has been a steady increase of interest in court reform. How much this movement owes to the inspiration of the *Journal of the American Judicature Society*, a beacon light in the cause of judicial reform for thirty-four years, cannot be overestimated. This gradual development of professional awareness of responsibility for putting the law in order, born perhaps of a sense of impending crisis in the law and in civilization, finds active expression among a relatively small but growing group of devoted judges and lawyers and alert laymen. They are the new leaders of the legal profession, who have gone steadily about the work of strengthening the law and the courts as essential elements in our civilization. Through their fine work more has been accomplished in improving the administration of justice in the last sixteen years than in the entire preceding century. In saying this, however, I am not suggesting that the millennium has arrived or even that it is just around the corner.

Without attempting to catalogue all the achievements of the last sixteen years, we may note that in 1938 for the first time the American Bar Association interested itself in the broad field of judicial administration by unanimously adopting as a standing program the numerous recommendations of its seven special Committees on Improving the Administration of Justice [6] and, equally important, that since then it has promoted its program for minimum standards of judicial administration year in and year out through its Section of Judicial Administration. The year 1938 also witnessed the adoption, after many years of travail, of the Federal Rules of Civil Procedure; and here it is significant to note that the promulgation of the original rules has been followed by continuous study and numerous amendments.[7] The Federal Rules of Criminal Procedure followed in due course in 1944, as have similar rules covering other branches of federal jurisdiction.[8] In 1939 came the establishment of the Administrative Office of the United States Courts,[9] a momentous advance which has since been followed in several jurisdictions.[10] In 1939 the

[6] 63 A.B.A. Rep. 516–656 (1938).

[7] 1939, 1946, 1948, 1951, Proposed Amendments of 1954 now pending.

[8] Clark, *Code Pleading* (2nd ed. 1947), Chap. 1, sec. 9.

[9] 28 U.S.C.A. secs. 444–447, now secs. 601–610.

[10] Cal., Colo., Conn., Iowa, Ky., La., Md., Mich., Mo., N.J., N.C., Ore., R.I., Va., D.C.; also Puerto Rico. For N.Y. see pp. 121–132 herein.

American Law Institute began work on its Model Code of Evidence, which was transformed in 1953 into the Uniform Rules of Evidence of the National Conference of Commissioners on Uniform State Laws and approved by the American Bar Association and the American Law Institute. In 1947 conservative New Jersey, and in 1947 and 1951 equally conservative Delaware, were the first American states to modernize not only their judicial structure and practice but also their administration, with the avowed purpose of eliminating technicalities, surprise, and delay; and a considerable number of other states are now struggling toward the same goal. But there was a vital distinction between the process in New Jersey, where, as in England a century before,[11] judicial reform came as a popular revolution won against the opposition of the bench and without the support of the organized bar, and that in Delaware, where the changes were the result of work by the bench and bar over a period of more than twenty years but without any pressure on the part of the public. In every state the bench primarily and the bar secondarily have the choice whether they or the people will lead in the inevitable modernization of system of courts and their procedure.

It is my hope that this little book will be useful to the judges, lawyers and laymen who are fighting the good fight for "the great interest of man on earth." The battlefield is a wide one and there are four sectors in particular that must be separately considered. They

[11] Sunderland, "The English Struggle for Procedural Reform," 39 *Harv. L. Rev.* 725 (1926).

vary widely with respect to the ease or difficulty of attaining victory. Fortunately for civilization and the law, in those sectors where the need is the greatest and most pressing, victory should prove to be easiest. The modernization and simplification of the substantive law is, of course, the most difficult task of all, and its achievement must necessarily await victory on the three other sectors of the battlefield. I shall discuss this in the last chapter, but first I shall discuss the three other sectors in the order of their importance today.

1. *The improvement of judicial personnel, including jurors as well as judges.* This is an exceedingly crucial problem in many jurisdictions, but one that is readily capable of solution everywhere.

2. *The simplification of the judicial structure and of procedure,* so that technicalities and surprise may be avoided, and so that procedure may become a means of achieving justice rather than an end in itself.

3. *The elimination of the law's delays by modern management methods and effective leadership.* Without these a judicial establishment cannot hope to function efficiently any more than any other statewide business. This calls for an administrative head of the courts in each jurisdiction and an administrative office of the courts to assist him.

CHAPTER II

Better Judges
and Better Jurors

THE basic consideration in every judicial establishment is the caliber of its personnel. The law as administered cannot be better than the judge who expounds it, the jurors who find the facts under the instructions of the judge as to the law, and the lawyers who try the case. Each must fulfill his function properly or a miscarriage of justice may ensue.

We need judges learned in the law, not merely the law in books but, something far more difficult to acquire, the law as applied in action in the courtroom; judges deeply versed in the mysteries of human nature and adept in the discovery of the truth in the discordant testimony of fallible human beings; judges beholden to no man, independent and honest and—equally important—believed by all men to be independent and honest; judges, above all, fired with consuming zeal to mete out justice according to law to every man, woman, and child that may come before them and to preserve individual freedom against any aggression of government; judges with the humility born of wisdom, patient and untiring in the search for truth and keenly conscious of the evils arising in a workaday world from any unnecessary delay. Judges with all of these attributes are not easy to find, but which of these traits dare we eliminate if we are to hope for evenhanded justice? Such ideal judges can after a fashion make even an inadequate system of substantive law achieve justice; on the other hand, judges who lack these qualifications will defeat the best system of substantive and procedural law imaginable.

Not less important is the need for jurors who represent a cross section of the honest and intelligent citizenry of the county and who are imbued with the solemnity of their function in the judicial process, and who are determined to perform their duty to the utmost of their ability. Similarly we must have lawyers who are competent, industrious, and ever mindful of their professional obligations as epitomized in the Canons of Professional Ethics, to present the facts to the court and jury and to argue the law to the court, for the law in operation is necessarily the joint product of the work of judge, jury, and counsel. Nor must we overlook the court clerks, the stenographic reporters, and the bailiffs whose integrity as well as whose skillful services are essential to the effective operation of the courts.

The struggle for an adequate and impartial judiciary in Anglo-American law has indeed been a long one. In England from an early date the courts were an adjunct of the executive. The royal courts, which superseded the local courts, were in name and in fact the king's courts and the judges served at the pleasure of the king. By Magna Carta, to be sure, King John covenanted that "We will appoint as justices . . . only such as know the law and mean duly to observe it well," [1] and by and large the English judges have always been learned in the law and experienced in court work, for they are regularly selected from among the leading barristers. Learning, however, is by no means the most important attribute of a judge. It required unusual courage for a judge to defy the wishes of a monarch who could dismiss him summarily. The fortitude of Lord Coke in standing up to James I on the question of the scope of the royal prerogative was indeed exceptional. It was not until 1700, following the Glorious Revolution, that the Act of Settlement was passed guaranteeing the independence of the judiciary by providing that the commissions of the judges should run during good behavior instead of merely at the king's pleasure.[2] The last vestige of dependence did not disappear until 1761, when a statute

[1] Chap. 45.

[2] 12 and 13 Wm. III, c. 2, sec. III (7); 1 Geo. III, c. 23; "Throughout the Stuart reigns judges have been dismissed if they withstand the king—too often they have been his servile creatures. All along they have held their offices *durante bene placito*—during the king's good pleasure. At once after the Revolution the question is raised, and William's judges were commissioned *quamdiu se bene gesserint*—during good behaviour. He, however, refused his assent to a bill for making this a matter of law—but the point was secured by the Act of Settlement (12 and 13 Will. III, c. 2). So soon as the House of Hanover comes to the throne judges' commissions are to be made *quamdiu se bene gesserint,* and their salaries are to be fixed, but they are to be removable upon an address of both houses of parliament. This means that a judge cannot be dismissed except either in consequence of a conviction of some offense, or on the address of both houses." Maitland, *The Constitutional History of England,* 312–313 (1931).

was finally passed providing that judges should continue in office notwithstanding the death of the king.[3]

The American colonies did not share in the blessing of an independent judiciary. In the Declaration of Independence the dissatisfaction of the colonists on this score was stated succinctly: "He [George III] has made judges dependent on his will alone, for the tenure of their offices, and the amount and payment of their salaries." [4] Accordingly, the original thirteen states did not follow the English method of judicial selection, nominally by the king, actually by the chancellor or prime minister, but with varying degrees of success made determined efforts to establish judicial systems that would be free of the abuses they had experienced. In only three of the states was the power of appointment vested in the governor subject to the consent of the council; [5] in two, appointments were made by the governor and the council; [6] and in the remaining eight states the power was vested in one or both houses of the legislature.[7] The term of office was for good behavior in eight states,[8] for fixed terms in three states,[9] at the pleasure of the general assembly in Georgia, while in Rhode Island the tenure was not clearly defined. Under our Federal Constitution the judges were appointed by the

[3] 1 Geo. III, c. 23.
[4] Ninth specification.
[5] Md., Mass., and N.Y.
[6] N.H. and Pa.
[7] Conn., Del., Ga., N.J., N.C., R.I., S.C., and Va.
[8] Del., Md., Mass., N.H., N.Y., N.C., S.C., and Va.
[9] Conn., 1 year; N.J., 7 and 5 years; Pa., 7 years.

President with the consent of the Senate and served during good behavior.[10] Thus in the postrevolutionary period in America we find that judges generally were selected by the executive or the legislature to serve in most instances during good behavior. Such a system was in accord with the philosophy prevailing in other civilized countries that the selection of impartial, honest judges learned in the law must be entrusted to a person or group capable of making an intelligent choice and that because of the professional qualifications demanded for judicial office the electorate as a whole cannot be expected to make such a choice intelligently any more than it could be expected, for instance, to select a surgeon general.

We have become so accustomed to the anomaly of elected judges that we will do well to remember that for the first three quarters of a century of our national history practically all of the judges were appointed, as they still are elsewhere in the civilized world. Except for justices of the peace and probate judges in some states, the only deviations from this principle before 1846 were the election of certain trial judges in Georgia beginning in 1812, and in Michigan beginning in 1836, and of associate circuit court judges but not the presidents of the circuit courts in Indiana beginning in 1816, as well as the election of all judges in Mississippi beginning in 1832. It was the change to elected judges in New York in 1846 that heralded the change to the popular election of all judges. By 1856 fifteen of the twenty-nine states existing

[10] U.S. Const. Art. 2, sec. 2; Art. 3, sec. 1.

in 1846 provided for the popular election of the judiciary, and in each of the states that have entered the Union since 1846 all or most of the judges are elected by the people for terms of years.[11] Only the relative unimportance at that time of the federal trial courts, the appointment of new justices in succession to Chief Justice Marshall and his associates, and the difficulty of amending the Federal Constitution saved the United States from an elective judiciary.

Today, with minor exceptions, the general situation is as follows: judges are appointed by the executive subject to confirmation in five states; judges are selected by the legislature in four; appellate judges are appointed under modified plans, with other judges elected, in two; trial judges are appointed by executive, and other judges are selected by popular or legislative vote in one; and all judges are elected in thirty-six. With respect to tenure, appellate judges are now in a preferred position over trial judges. Appellate judges hold office for life during good behavior in three states; for life during good behavior on reappointment after an initial term of seven years in one state; for a term of ten years or longer in fourteen states; for a term of five years or more but less than ten in twenty-nine states; and for a term of less than five years only in one state. Trial judges hold office during good behavior in three states; during good behavior on reappointment following an initial term of seven years in one state; for terms of ten years or more in only four states; for a term of five years or more but

[11] Haynes, *Selection and Tenure of Judges* 100 (1944).

less than ten in twenty-five states; and for terms of less than five years in fifteen states.[12]

Judges elected by the people are not only unknown in any other English-speaking common-law country but everywhere else except Soviet Russia and its satellites, a dubious distinction of which we cannot be proud.[13] How did this situation come about? The key to an understanding of our present-day problems with a judiciary elected by the people is to be found in the popular revolt of the second quarter of the nineteenth century, often called the Jacksonian Revolution. This movement swept away whatever aristocratic pretensions of Federalism may have lingered on through the Jeffersonian era, including respect for the learned professions, and gave a new meaning to many of the concepts of the earlier Jeffersonian democratic political philosophy. Jefferson believed that all men were created equal, but the plain people of the Jacksonian era went much farther and boldly proclaimed that all men are in fact equal. The practical application of this philosophy resulted in the antiprofessionalism of the period, with devastating effects on the bar, especially in the recruitment of new members under lowered standards of admission or in some states no standards at all. The new notions of equality in fact were applied in the selection of judges, resulting in an inferior judiciary in the second half of the nineteenth century. Once it was assumed as a working

[12] Vanderbilt, ed., *Minimum Standards of Judicial Administration,* 17–21 (1949).
[13] Cf. Soviet Constitution, Article 105.

premise that all men are in fact equal, one could reach some very startling results which inevitably had their effect upon the courts. Thus, if all men were in fact equal, it must necessarily follow that all lawyers, being men, were also equal, and that all judges, likewise being men, were likewise equal. If one smiles at this line of thought, I ask you if it does not serve to explain the practice of the rotation of the chief justiceship in seventeen states of the Union to this very day.[14] Two states even shift their chief justice every six months! [15]

This fundamental premise of the Jacksonian pioneer doctrine also goes far to account for the attitude of trial judges of the frontier toward the reviewing tribunal at the state capitol. Every judge—indeed, every public official—was deemed an equal of every other, though assigned different duties. None would brook control or even supervision by another as a normal routine. Each was self-sufficient, being brought to account in event of default of his fulfillment of his public duties only by legal proceedings to review his action or inaction, or at the worst, by impeachment. The adverse effect of the dogma of equality in fact, however, was not confined to the appellate tribunals. It plagued even the trial judges, for if all men are equal, lawyers and judges are necessarily equal. This might account for some of the strange deportment that disgraced many a courtroom in the mid-nineteenth century.[16] Even worse so far as the

[14] Vanderbilt, *op. cit.* 34.
[15] Ind., Iowa.
[16] Dickens, *American Notes* 62–4 (1907).

judges were concerned, the equality of the lawyers with them gave the lawyers an equal right to aspire to judicial office. The only way that this right could be achieved was to reduce tenure to short terms. The office, of course, should be elective, because it would not do, all the citizens being equal to the governor, to permit the governor to appoint the judges. By some such line of reasoning as this, though probably not syllogistic in form, and because of a desire to make the judges responsive to the people, the political philosophy of rotation in office was applied to the judiciary and in most states coupled with the new slogan: "To the victor belong the spoils." And so in the era that followed, the judges campaigned for judicial office on the hustings with the other candidates of the political parties from sheriff to hog-reeve. It was not conceded that it required any special training or qualifications to be a judge. President Andrew Jackson expressed the popular idea as to all public offices in his first annual message:

> "There are, perhaps, few men who can for any great length of time enjoy office and power without being more or less under the influence of feelings unfavorable to the faithful discharge of their public duties. . . . The duties of all public officers are, or at least admit of being made, so plain and simple that men of intelligence may readily qualify themselves for their performance; and I cannot but believe that more is lost by the long continuance of men in office than is generally to be gained by their experience. I submit,

therefore, to your consideration whether the efficiency of the government would not be promoted, and official industry and integrity better secured, by a general extension of the law which limits appointments to four years." [17]

Before proceeding to discuss the present-day effects of the Jacksonian Revolution on the courts, we must pause to note three major attacks on the courts, all of which fortunately proved abortive. President Jefferson and his followers in Congress all took violent exception to the decision in *Marbury v. Madison* [18] enunciating the power of the Supreme Court to declare an act of Congress null and void as violative of the Constitution. Jefferson's attacks on the federal judiciary and especially on his cousin, Chief Justice Marshall, were continual. His adherents, led by Senator Giles of Virginia, expressed the view that it was the duty of the courts to conform to the wishes of the people as expressed in legislation. Senator Giles declared that "a removal by impeachment was nothing more than a declaration by Congress to this effect: 'You hold dangerous opinions, and if you are suffered to carry them into effect, you will work the destruction of the nation. We want your offices for the purpose of giving them the men who will fill them better.' " [19] This view doubtless had its origin in the

[17] December 8, 1829, in Thorpe, *The Statesmanship of Andrew Jackson*, 35, 44–5 (1909).
[18] 5 U.S. 137, 2 L. ed. 60 (1803).
[19] 3 Beveridge, *The Life of John Marshall*, 158.

English practice in preceding centuries of using the impeachment process to get rid of an undesirable minister. Such were the weaknesses of Justice Samuel Chase that his impeachment was the grand opportunity of the adherents of Jefferson to put these views into effect, but fortunately for the country and the place of the judiciary in enforcing the rule of law, Senator Giles shifted ground and the impeachment of Justice Chase failed by a narrow margin. The second attack came in the early part of this century, when Theodore Roosevelt and his Progressive party urged first the recall of judges and then the recall of judicial decisions, either of which would have been far more destructive of judicial independence than the changes foisted on the courts by the Jacksonian reformers. Finally, in 1936 President Franklin D. Roosevelt undertook his ill-fated court-packing plan, aiming at executive control of the Supreme Court to obtain decisions to his liking. Both of these attacks on the independence of the courts were defeated by the mobilization of public opinion largely through the efforts of the American Bar Association.

The full effects of the Jacksonian elective system did not begin to be felt at once. Indeed, the evil was not generally recognized until the latter half of the nineteenth century, first in the larger cities such as New York where partisan judges controlled by men like Boss Tweed were elected to office. The situation would be quite intolerable in such places and perhaps elsewhere did not on the average about a third of the judges, often lawyers of superior attainments, reach the bench through *ad interim* executive appointment to fill vacancies caused by death or resignation. These temporary appointments enabled them in many instances to make a successful contest for election for a full term. In some states with a stable population and a responsible bar the elective system has seemed to work well, especially in the appellate courts, but in most states the elective system all too often drives the judges into active politics with the commitments politics entails. Not only are aspirants for judicial office forced to campaign along with numerous other candidates on political slates, but in many states they are the unofficial but actual party leaders, especially at the county level; indeed they must be, if they hope to be reelected. In violation of the Canons of Judicial Ethics, in some states they participate openly in local and state political conventions and even in national conventions. Thus in Pennsylvania eight judges were members of a national nominating convention in 1952. Four years before that the then chief justice ran as a delegate; when his ethical right to do so without first resigning his judicial position was challenged, he retorted by calling one of his opponents a skunk and a moron.[20] It is impossible to

[20] "Maxey, announcing the decision of his associates [that he might continue to hear cases from Lackawanna County notwithstanding his candidacy], issued a statement attacking Leach. 'Leach's telegraphic request is based on nothing but envy and malice,' Maxey said. 'I refuse to enter into a personal controversy with him because no self-respecting man engages in a physical contest with a skunk or a mental contest with a moron. A case like Leach's should be dealt with by a psychiatrist, and there is not much that even a psychiatrist could do with a problem case

determine how widespread this practice is because the reports on national conventions classify "judges and lawyers" in a single category,[21] from which one might infer that the practice is not uncommon. Of a piece with such activities is the practice, in states where judges are elected, of their running for nonjudicial offices without resigning from the bench.[22] In some states, moreover, the reported campaign contributions made by and on behalf of judicial candidates run into large figures; for example in a recent California primary campaign the reported expenses of some judicial candidates exceeded their annual salaries.[23]

The history of the Canons of Judicial Ethics reveals the inevitable conflict between a judge's performance of his ethical obligations to refrain from all forms of political activity and the necessity of his being in politics, if he is to be reelected in a state with the elective system. Until 1933 Canon 28 read as follows:

"While entitled to entertain his personal views of political questions, and while not required to surrender his rights or opinions as a citizen, it is inevitable that

---

like Leach's. If the venom in Leach's heart ever spills over into his stomach, his demise will be immediate. If the share of the milk of human decency which the Creator alloted to Leach was churned, it would yield nothing but Limburger cheese.' " *Phila. Evening Bulletin,* April 21, 1948.

[21] Meadows and Braucher, "Social Composition of the 1948 National Convention," 36 *Sociology and Social Research* 31, 34 (Sept.–Oct. 1951).

[22] Drinker, *Legal Ethics* (1953), p. 279; A.B.A. op. 193.

[23] *Daily Palo Alto Times,* June 25, 1954.

suspicion of being warped by political bias will attach to a judge who becomes the active promoter of the interests of one political party as against another. He should avoid making political speeches, making or soliciting payment of assessments or contributions to party funds, the public endorsement of candidates for political office and participation in party conventions." [24]

Who can doubt the soundness of its admonitions or its comprehensiveness in seeking to prohibit all forms of political activity? The canon, however, did not succeed in attaining its objective, and in 1933 an effort was made to strengthen it by adding: "He should neither accept nor retain a place on any party committee nor act as party leader, nor engage generally in partisan activities." [25]

Here again the soundness of every word of the amendment from the standpoint of achieving a judiciary both independent and believed to be independent seems obvious. The canon was again amended in 1950 but this time weakened by adding: "Where, however, it is necessary for judges to be nominated and elected as candidates of a political party, nothing herein contained shall prevent the judge from attending or speaking at political gatherings, or from making contributions to the campaign funds of the party that has nominated him and seeks his election or reelection." [26]

[24] 48 A.B.A. Rep. 459 (1923).
[25] 58 A.B.A. Rep. 718 (1933).
[26] 75 A.B.A. Rep. 121 (1950).

This amendment recognizes the predicament that confronts a judge, barred by the canon in the form in which it stood before 1950 from participation in any form of politics, who was obliged to run for reelection against an opponent or opponents who have no such prohibition binding them. The amendment, nevertheless, takes the teeth out of the canon as a whole in states that elect their judges. How is it possible for a judge driven to do the things permitted by the 1950 amendment to achieve the same reputation for independence and integrity that would be possible were he free from all political activities? If a judge may attend and speak at political meetings and make political contributions, what assurance has the public that the relationship ends there? The wonder is that such a system has produced as many distinguished judges as it has.

What the effect of political activities and of substantial campaign contributions may be on the judicial mind it is impossible to state with accuracy—it will doubtless vary in different states and with different judges—but the collective effect of these matters on the public mind may be gauged from a nationwide Gallup poll taken in 1939,[27] the results of which were tabulated as follows:

In general, do you think judges in the
Federal courts of the country are
honest?   Yes 86%

In general, do you think judges in the
state courts are honest?   Yes 76%

[27] 3 *Public Opinion Quarterly* 581, 595 (1939).

In general, do you think judges in the
municipal or local courts are honest?   Yes 72%

The fact that only 76% of those answering the poll
thought that the judges in the state courts were honest as
against 86% who thought the judges in the federal
courts were honest is evidence that cannot be ignored.
How can we account for the relatively low standing of
state court judges and especially of municipal or local
judges? Is the cause due in part to the political activities
of state judges in states with the elective system? Even
more fundamental, how can we account for the doubts
in the minds of so many people as to the honesty of all
types of judges, however selected? Is it due in part to
politics in the selection of appointed judges as well as
elected judges? The damning point is not whether so
many citizens are correct in their lack of confidence in
their courts. The gravity of the situation resides in the
very existence of this lack of confidence. Nothing that
has happened since 1939 would lead one to suspect that
the situation has improved in the intervening fifteen
years since the poll was taken. Obviously the first task
of the bar in every state should be to ascertain whether
the results of the poll still hold true and especially
whether there is the same differential between the popular views with respect to federal judges and state judges
now as there was in 1939. If there is, the bar of the state
has a grave duty which it must bring itself to face. If the
fountain of justice has been polluted or is believed by
many to be polluted, the bar of a state can have no

greater responsibility than to remove the cause of contamination or believed contamination and to prevent its recurrence.

Regardless of the method of selection, we cannot hope to make much real progress in improving the caliber of the judiciary until we have a simple understandable declaration of the qualifications and attributes of a good appellate judge, a good trial judge, and a good local magistrate, so that those who are responsible for the selection of judges may have adequate standards by which to measure candidates for judicial office. Much of our difficulty in this field, I believe, springs from the fact that all too few people, whether in public life or as private citizens, have ever given much thought to what they should be seeking when it comes to choosing their judges. If they understood what traits and what experience it takes to do a good job in this very difficult profession, they would probably make their choices more intelligently than they often do. Indeed, thoughtful consideration of the problem would lead them eventually to desire to improve the method of judicial selection. Such a declaration as I have in mind would be no more difficult to formulate than the Canons of Judicial Ethics; the only difference would be that the proposed declaration would deal with traits and experience necessary to equip a lawyer to go on the bench rather than with the rules governing his conduct once he is on the bench. I have already mentioned some of the necessary characteristics of a good judge, but at this point I should like to add another: a demonstrated willingness to improve judicial procedure and administration.

Nor should I eliminate political experience as a qualification for judicial office. Politics is such a large part of American life that a judge who does not understand it is likely to make many blunders until he learns what it is all about. But once on the bench he must cease to be a politician. Mr. Justice Lummus of the Massachusetts Supreme Court has put it tersely: "There is no certain harm in turning a politician into a judge. He may be or become a good judge. The curse of the elective system is the converse, that it turns almost every judge into a politician." [28]

In suggesting that a knowledge of or experience in politics is an asset to a judge provided he ceases to practice it on becoming a judge, I would not be understood as advocating the selection of judges by presidents, governors, or party leaders as political rewards—far from it. The admitted superiority of English judges may be traced to the fact, first, that they are chosen from the select group of Queen's Counsel, all barristers with years of courtroom experience and, second, that they are chosen primarily for their professional and not their political qualifications. Especially impressive and almost unbelievable in America, where judgeships are all too often regarded as political prizes under both the elective and appointive systems, is the statement of former Lord Chancellor Jowitt that during his six years in office he did not appoint a single member of his party (the Labour Party) to a judgeship.

[28] Lummus, *The Trial Judge*, 138 (1937).

Having determined what should be required of our judges and having formulated these requirements in a declaration that everyone can understand, the next task is to find the body that can best measure each candidate for judicial selection to ascertain the degree to which he conforms to the standards laid down in the declaration. The lawyers of the community have daily opportunities to observe the character and the professional qualifications of their fellow-lawyers seeking judicial appointment for the first time and of judges themselves seeking another term in office. The bar is therefore in a better position than any other group to evaluate a candidate's judicial ability. Accordingly, whether judges are appointed or elected, the members of the organized bar manifestly have the clear duty as citizens, as well as a professional responsibility as lawyers, to advise the appointing authority or the electorate of their informed and unbiased opinion of each candidate's fitness. This opportunity has been utilized to a certain degree at every level of government, but unfortunately in many instances either from inadequate leadership in the bar or from lack of courage this great opportunity for improving judicial selections has not been fully employed as it should be. The organized bar should urge the choice of the best available candidate on the selecting power whether the selection is to be made by the president or a governor or by the legislature or by the people or, in those states where the party organizations control, by the party leaders. This is a function of the bar that requires great courage, and in a number of states it may even be necessary to call outstanding laymen to the aid of the bar, since in many states the organized bar has been slow to sense its responsibility in this matter.

The publication of a declaration of judicial qualifications and the active leadership of the bar and interested laymen could lead in many states to a change in the method of judicial selection in favor of executive appointment under what is known as the American Bar plan.[29] This plan is also called the Missouri [30] plan because it is used in the selection of appellate judges in that state, as a device to overcome the weaknesses of the elective system. A variation of it is used in California.[31] The American Bar plan is a very real advance over the elective system; it is the best possible plan where for one reason or another the appointive method is not available. Essentially it is a plan whereby a judge runs, not against an opponent, but against his own record. It was aptly described in the resolution of the House of Delegates of the American Bar Association adopting it in 1937:

"RESOLVED, By the House of Delegates of the American Bar Association, That in its judgment the following plan offers the most acceptable substitute available for direct election of judges:

(a) The filling of vacancies by appointment by the executive or other elective official or officials, but from a list named by another agency, composed in part of

[29] 62 A.B.A. Rep. 1033 (1937).
[30] Mo. Const. Art. V, par. 29.
[31] Cal. Const. Art. VI, Sec. 26.

high judicial officers and in part of other citizens, selected for the purpose, who hold no other public office.

(b) If further check upon appointment be desired, such check may be supplied by the requirement of confirmation by the State Senate or other legislative body of appointments made through the dual agency suggested.

(c) The appointee after a period of service should be eligible for reappointment periodically thereafter, or periodically go before the people upon his record, with no opposing candidate, the people voting upon the question 'Shall Judge Blank be retained in office?' "

Whenever an incompetent judge seeks another term under the American Bar plan, an alert bar is forewarned and can act effectively to warn the people; this has not always been possible in states with an elective system where the entrenched power of a political organization has willed otherwise. Under the Amerian Bar plan the power of the people to reelect a judge is real and not illusory, as it is in elections and reelections of judges in jurisdictions where the political parties dominate nominations and elections. How illusory this right of the people is can be illustrated by the fact that at the election held on November 2, 1954, the people in New York County were called upon to vote for four judges of the Court of Appeals, eight of the Supreme Court, two in the Court of General Sessions, three in the Municipal Court, and four in the City Court. Manifestly it is impossible for the average citizen to pass intelligently upon the qualifications of the many candidates for this many judgeships, to say nothing of the problems of choosing candidates for nonjudicial offices.

Even under the appointive system the organized bar frequently does not become aware of an individual's candidacy until the appointment is announced, or it may not be able to convene quickly enough to take appropriate action. Some active associations have made efforts to persuade the appointing authority to consult with them in advance of appointments, but with varying success. Where an appointment is subject to confirmation, however, an opportunity is afforded for vigorous protest against a poor selection, but it is obviously a last line of defense against an unwise appointment and often it comes too late. In New Jersey the Governor, who makes judicial appointments subject to the confirmation by the Senate, is required to give seven days' public notice of his intention to submit a judicial appointment to the Senate for confirmation, thus giving the bar and other interested persons time to make known to him, the Senate, and the public any facts adverse to the prospective nominee.[32] Massachusetts has a similar salutary provision requiring judicial nominations to be made by the Governor at least seven days before action by the Council.[33] Such provisions are helpful.

There is another principle of judicial selection the

[32] N.J. Const. Art. VI, sec. 6, par. 1.
[33] Mass. Const. Part II, c. 2., sec. 1, Art. IX.

wisdom of which cannot be stressed too strongly. I refer
to a bipartisan judiciary such as the Delaware Constitution [34] provides and such as New Jersey has enjoyed for
a century as a matter of unbroken tradition without
constitutional or statutory compulsion. A bipartisan
system insures that at least half of the judges will not
be appointed for political considerations, but rather because they are competent lawyers with judicial tempera-
ment. Because of this practice, moreover, the judges in
Delaware and New Jersey are not exposed to the danger
of not being reappointed simply because the governor in
office at the time they come up for reappointment hap-
pens to belong to the opposite political party. An even
more important effect of such a practice is that the decisions of a bipartisan court in cases which are of political
importance have more weight with the profession and
the public, especially if the decisions are unanimous or
substantially so, than would the decisions of a court
chosen exclusively or preponderantly from one political
party. Paradoxical though it may sound, a bipartisan
judiciary is the only way in this country to achieve a
nonpartisan judiciary, and who would deny that all justice should be nonpartisan?

In stressing the necessity for good judges we must not
overlook the significance of the jury. A single unintelli-
gent juror, however honest, or a single dishonest juror,
however intelligent, may undo the work of the ablest
judge and most conscientious counsel. The selection of

[34] Del. Const. Art. IV. sec. 3.

jurors is therefore a matter of prime importance to both litigants and the state. There are twenty-four states in which the jury panels are selected by politically elected officials and in such states there is always the danger and generally the reality that the jury panel will be selected with political considerations in mind. Jury panels should always be selected by the judges (provided, of course, the existing system of judicial selection insures judges free from politics) or by commissioners selected for this purpose by the judges, and such jury commissioners should be chosen on a bipartisan basis and should be entirely divorced from politics.[35] I remember the reply of a United States Senator to my plea to him years ago for his support of a bill authorizing the courts to appoint jury commissioners to select the jury panels; he had no objection to such a method of selection in civil cases in New Jersey, but he would tolerate no change in the political selection of jurors in criminal matters—one could never tell when one would need help! The danger is obvious and the cure is simple: a statute giving the court the power to appoint bipartisan jury commissioners, empowered to select jurors who represent a cross section of the honest and intelligent citizenry of the county. The jury should be chosen on a nonpartisan basis for relatively short terms of service, such as two weeks, so as not to prove a burden to the individual juror. The responsibility of the bar here is as great as it is for the selection of good judges. The wonder is that

[35] A.B.A. Section of Judicial Administration Handbook, *The Improvement of the Administration of Justice* (3rd ed., 1952), 66.

the matter has not been attended to long since in every state.

Much might be said of the responsibilities of the individual lawyer and of the organized bar to the law, to the courts, and to clients, but to do so would take us far afield. The sphere of the responsibility of the profession is constantly growing. What the public is expecting of us has been set forth in several recent bar surveys of public relations, but there is no responsibility of the individual lawyer or of the organized profession that can match in importance or in immediacy the duty to preserve the judicial system from taint or suspicion of taint and to improve the administration of justice by improving the caliber of judges and jurors. This responsibility is the foremost challenge of "things as they are" to the profession. With the gradual development of new leadership in the profession, the flame of progress is again being kindled and we may look forward with confidence to the solution of a fundamental problem in the courts that has heretofore been discussed only behind closed doors or in veiled language.

CHAPTER III

Simplified Judicial
Structure and Procedure

I SHALL now attempt to show how the law has in certain jurisdictions at least thrown off the shackles of complicated court systems, of technicalities and fictions in procedure and pleadings, and of irrational restrictions on the use of available evidence, and how it has substituted instead a simple court structure, flexible rules of procedure aiming at the elimination of technicalities and of surprise, and finally the shortening and improvement of trials by pretrial conferences and modernized rules of evidence. All this, however, is a mere beginning. In every state there must still be an intensive study of every phase of procedural law on a comparative basis, in order to make them so effective that litigants will prefer to resort to the courts rather than to commercial arbitration and administrative tribunals.

Over the centuries what we call Anglo-American freedom for the individual has been won partly on the field of battle, partly in legislative halls, but for the most part in the courts of law. It constitutes the great contribution of lawyers and judges to our civilization and to human happiness. Much of this contribution has come in the form of improvements in procedure, but singularly enough to no branch of the law is the profession so generally allergic as to procedure. This is all the more unfortunate because skill in the use of procedure is one of the chief weapons in the lawyer's armory for solving the practical problems of the law. Yet professional allergy to procedure is nothing new; it has affected the entire history of Anglo-American efforts to redress individual and public wrongs not only with respect to pleadings, procedure generally, and methods of trial, but also with reference to the jurisdiction of the courts.

The number of courts known to the common law is astounding. Coke devotes his entire *Fourth Institute* [1] to a description of the courts of his time: "So many distinct courts," he moans, "above the number of one hundred." [2] At the end of his comprehensive volume this arch conservative of the law quotes with approval the aphorism of Plowden, "Blessed be the amending hand." [3] Like all of Coke's writing, the *Fourth Institute* is not easy reading; the history of the jurisdiction of the English courts brought down to date may be found in more attractive form in the first volume of Holdsworth's monumental *History of English Law*.[4] But even this great work, which is as orderly as Coke's is unsystematic, will, I fear, weary all but the most ardent students of law, so complicated and confused was the judicial structure it portrays. It is almost unbelievable that de-

[1] (1642).
[2] *ibid.*, 365.
[3] *ibid.*, 366.
[4] 3d ed. (1922).

spite the plea of Coke for a simplification of the English court system and despite the inconvenience, expense, and delay that resulted for centuries from its complexities and anachronisms, not much was done to relieve the situation—except the abortive attempt of Lord Chief Justice Mansfield in the latter part of the eighteenth century to merge law and equity [5]—until the Judicature Act of 1873. Until then there were, among many other courts, three great separate common-law courts competing with each other for business—the Queen's Bench, the Common Pleas and the Court of Exchequer—while the Court of Chancery had its own peculiar jurisdiction that was constantly colliding with them. The Judicature Acts brought order out of a chaos in which litigants had been obliged for centuries to shuttle back and forth between law and equity and to take particular kinds of suits to particular courts.[6] This fundamental reform, it is interesting to observe, was brought about not by the bench or bar, but by laymen led by a few, a very few, courageous judges and lawyers.

While we have never had as many distinct courts as existed in England prior to the Judicature Acts, still it is interesting to observe that as late as 1947 New Jersey had seventeen courts or parts of courts.[7] Nor was New Jersey unique, for there are still many states that have complicated judicial systems comprised of courts with

---

[5] Fifoot, *Lord Mansfield*, 183–197 (1936).

[6] Maitland, *The Constitutional History of England*, 471 (1931).

[7] Woelper, "The Reorganization of the Judiciary in New Jersey," *1 Sidney L. Rev.* 46 (1953).

overlapping and conflicting jurisdictions far beyond the necessities of the situation, established either by constitutions or statutes or even ordinances. Indeed, there is reason to doubt that many lawyers in many of the states in the Union could without study enumerate all of the courts of their state and describe their jurisdiction. All that is needed for an adequate court organization today is, first, a trial court of general statewide jurisdiction over all matters—civil, criminal, equitable, and probate; and, second, a court to hear appeals, and if the size of the state and the volume of its judicial business require it, an intermediate court or courts of appeal; and, third, chiefly as a matter of convenience, a local court to hear petty civil and criminal matters and to bind defendants over for the grand jury. The English courts and the federal courts follow substantially this model, but very few of the states have such a simple system or anything approaching it, though there can be no justification for a complicated system of courts other than the chronic professional inability to see the need of any kind of change in the law, especially when it affects judges and lawyers in their work. The need for a simplified court structure, if we are to avoid the conflicts of jurisdiction that plague litigants and if we are to achieve efficiency in operation, is second only in importance to improving the caliber of judges and jurors. Yet this obviously necessary reform has been accomplished only in the federal courts, California, Delaware, New Jersey, and Puerto Rico.

Even more fantastic than the complicated congeries

of courts was the involved system of procedure that developed both at law and in equity over the centuries in the shape of a confused agglomeration of precedents, rules of court, fictions, and statutes. Blackstone, writing in Olympian detachment from the workaday world, could seek to justify the procedure of his day by fine language which nevertheless concedes its shortcomings:

"Our system of remedial law resembles an old Gothic castle, erected in the days of chivalry, but fitted up for a modern inhabitant. The moated ramparts, the embattled towers, and the trophied halls, are magnificent and venerable; but useless, and therefore neglected. The inferior apartments, now accommodated to daily use, are cheerful and commodious, though their approaches may be winding and difficult." [8]

Such an edifice could not hope to survive in an age of science and business efficiency. Any lawyer of antiquarian bent who is interested in the mass of outmoded learning that governed the daily work of the bench and bar for centuries may find it embalmed in the stout volumes of Tidd's *Practice*,[9] Chitty on *Pleading*,[10] and Daniell on *Equity Pleading and Practice*.[11] Why intelligent men should have tolerated such intricate nonsense for centuries and made no effort to shake themselves free of it is difficult to explain, except by our inveterate

[8] 3 *Bl. Comm.* 268 (1765–1769).
[9] 1st ed. 1790–1794, 4th U.S. ed., 1856.
[10] 1st ed. 1809, 16th U.S. ed., 1892.
[11] 1st ed. 1837–1841, 8th ed. 1914.

aversion to change. We may smile at the successive efforts to compel a defendant to appear in court, varying in stringency from a polite summons to a decree of outlawry, when all we now do is to serve him or a member of his family with a summons and complaint and then, if he fails to answer within the prescribed time, to take judgment against him by default, but it took nearly six centuries to correct the primitive notion that the power of a court to act depended upon the defendant's appearance in court.[12] But we find it more difficult to justify the subtleties of special pleading which dominated actions at law in England for centuries up to the time of the Judicature Acts. Lord Chief Justice Coleridge in recounting his early days at the bar describes the situation vividly:

"The system [special pleading] had its great virtues, but it had its great and crying evils; and they were aggravated by the powerful men who at that time dominated Westminster Hall, and whose spirit guided its administration. . . . The ruling power in the Courts in 1847 was Baron Parke, a man of great and wide legal learning, an admirable scholar, a kind-hearted and amiable man, and of remarkable force of mind. These great qualities he devoted to heightening all the absurdities, and contracting to the very utmost the narrowness of the system of special pleading. The client was unthought of. Conceive a judge rejoicing, as I have myself heard Baron Parke rejoice, at non-

[12] 2 Holdsworth, *op. cit.*, 104, 105.

suiting a plaintiff in an undefended cause, saying, with
a sort of triumphant air, that 'those who drew loose
declarations brought scandal on the law.' The right
was nothing, the mode of stating everything. When it
was proposed to give power to amend the statement,
'Good Heavens,' exclaimed the Baron, 'think of the
state of the Record!'—i.e., the sacred parchment,
which it was proposed to defile by erasures and altera-
tions. He bent the whole powers of his great intellect
to defeat the Act of Parliament which had allowed of
equitable defences in a Common Law action. He laid
down all but impossible conditions, and said, with an
air of intense satisfaction, in my hearing, 'I think we
settled the new Act to-day, we shall hear no more of
Equitable defences'! And as Baron Parke piped, the
Court of Exchequer followed, and dragged after it,
with more or less reluctance, the other Common Law
Courts of Westminster Hall. . . . Even so very
great a lawyer and so independent a man as Sir James
Willes dedicated a book to him as the judge 'to whom
the law was under greater obligations than to any
judge within legal memory.' One of the obligations he
was very near conferring on it was its absolute extinc-
tion. 'I have aided in building up sixteen volumes of
Meeson & Welsby,' said he proudly to Charles Austin, 'and that is a great thing for any man to say,' 'I
dare say it is,' said Austin, 'but in the Palace of Truth,
Baron, do you think it would have made the slightest
difference to mankind, or even to England, if all the
cases in all the volumes of Meeson & Welsby had been

decided the other way?' He repeated his boast to Sir William Erle. 'It's a lucky thing,' said Sir William, as he told me himself, 'that there was not a seventeenth volume, for if there had been the Common Law itself would have disappeared altogether, amidst the jeers and hisses of mankind;' 'and,' he added, 'Parke didn't seem to like it.'

"Peace be with him. He was a great lawyer, a man of high character and powerful intellect. No smaller man could have produced such results. If he ever were to revisit the glimpses of the moon one shudders to think of his disquiet. No absque hoc, no et non, no colour, express or implied, given to trespass, no new assignment, belief in the great doctrine of a negative pregnant no longer necessary to legal salvation, and the very nice question, as Baron Parke is reported to have thought, whether you could reply de injuria to a plea of deviation in an action on the marine policy not only still unsolved, but actually considered not worth solution! I suspect that to the majority of my hearers I am talking in an unknown tongue, and it is strange that in the lifetime of one who has not yet quite fulfilled the appointed span of human life such a change, such a revolution in a most conservative profession should be actually consummated." [13]

What a revolution it was I know from experience, because special pleading, although eliminated in some states as much as a century before the English reforms,

[13] 37 *Contemporary Rev.* 799–801 (June, 1890).

was still in vogue in New Jersey [14] when I began to study law.

All of this is quite beyond our understanding today unless we remember that through the centuries when the English law was developing in the royal courts, the jurisdiction of the law courts was not a general one, but that the courts obtained jurisdiction in each individual case through an original writ specifying a type of action which issued out of the chancery office [15] under the great seal. If a plaintiff were so unfortunate as to select a writ that did not suit the facts as they developed at his trial he was inevitably nonsuited, even though the very facts he proved at the trial would have supported some other writ.[16] Such were the happy hunting grounds of Baron Parke and his confreres, and even of some of the early American judges whose actions illustrated the old adage that a little learning is dangerous. In their desire to ape all things English and to follow the niceties of English procedure, they ran counter to popular feeling that this was not justice. Their actions led to statutes altering procedure and incorporating reforms,[17] thus paving the way for the legislature to take over the control of procedure.

Equally inexplicable to us today are the old modes of

[14] Superseded by N. J. Practice Act (1912).

[15] Sutton, *Personal Actions at Common Law,* Chap. 2, "The Original Writs" (1929).

[16] Odgers, "Changes in Procedure and in the Law of Evidence," in *A Century of Law Reform,* 203, 212–213 (1901).

[17] Field, "Law Reform in the United States and its Influence Abroad," 25 *Am. L. Rev.* 515 (1891).

trial. I have in mind not so much the reliance in the early centuries on the appeal to the supernatural in trials by ordeal, by battle, and by wager of law, for to our ancestors the powers of heaven and hell were very real indeed,[18] but rather the artificial restrictions imposed by the courts on the kind of evidence they would permit to go to the jury. Again let me quote Lord Chief Justice Coleridge:

"Truth was investigated by rules of evidence so carefully framed to exclude falsehood, that very often truth was quite unable to force its way through the barriers erected against its opposite. Plantiff and defendant, husband and wife, persons, excepting Quakers, who objected to an oath, those with an interest, direct or indirect, immediate or contingent, in the issue to be tried, were all absolutely excluded from giving evidence. Nonsuits were constant, not because there was no cause of action, but because the law refused the evidence of the only persons who could prove it." [19]

All of these restrictions disappeared piecemeal. In 1843 by Act of Parliament persons other than parties to a case were allowed to testify; [20] in 1846 parties were allowed to testify in the English county courts [21] and in 1851 in all courts in civil suits; [22] but it was not until

[18] Maitland, *op. cit.,* 119–120.
[19] 37 *Contemporary Rev.* 798 (June, 1890).
[20] Lord Denman's Act, 1843 (6 and 7 Vict., c. 85).
[21] 9 and 10 Vict. c. 95.
[22] Law of Evidence Amendment Act (14 and 15 Vict. c. 99).

1898 [23] that a defendant was allowed, though not compelled, to testify in a criminal suit. It is difficult for us to realize that it was not until a century ago (1854) that an English judge was given power to hear a common law case without a jury.[24] In this country progress in the law of evidence has been stimulated by the scholarship of Thayer, Wigmore, and Morgan, culminating in the Uniform Rules of Evidence previously referred to, which are now awaiting acceptance, I hope, in the several states.

So much for the procedure, pleadings, and methods of trial in the courts of law before the Judicature Acts. When the formulation of new original writs ceased by reason of administrative conservatism (despite the mandate of the Statute of Westminster II [25] to issue them in cases similar to those which had been issued before) and when the use of fictions to adapt old writs to new uses had been pushed to the limit, the processes of the law would inevitably have broken down had not new principles come to the aid of the common law with both new remedies and new substantive rights enforced in the Court of Chancery in the name of equity and good conscience. But sound and beneficent though the substantive body of equitable principles was, and efficient as was its remedy by injunction once it was ordered, its procedure unfortunately became even more cumbersome, tedious, expensive, and frustrating than the meth-

[23] 61 and 62 Vict. c. 36.
[24] 17 and 18 Vict. c. 125, sec. 1.
[25] (1283).

ods of the law courts. Since for centuries the chancellors were learned ecclesiastics administering sound morality in the name of the law, one would not expect to see the procedural absurdities of the common law repeated, but the chancellors quite naturally employed the procedure of the ecclesiastical law used in the courts Christian, and ecclesiastical procedure unfortunately was even worse than common law procedure.[26]

An original bill in chancery (there were three kinds of bills, but we can pause only to glance at the principal one) contained nine parts of which only the third, stating the plaintiff's case, was necessary. The Reverend John Wesley called it quite properly: "that foul monster, a Chancery Bill, . . . stuffed with such stupid senseless improbable lies; many of them, too, quite foreign to the question, as I believe would have cost the compiler his life in any Heathen Court either of Greece or Rome." [27] There were nine grounds of demurrer and fourteen pleas to a bill, but they were seldom available if the bill was properly drawn. The answer under oath was likewise technical. If the plaintiff thought it insufficient, he took exception to it and compelled fuller answers.

The only good thing that could be said of equity pleading was that through it a plaintiff could obtain a statement under oath from the defendant of the truth or falsity of the plaintiff's allegations, something that the

[26] Odgers, *op. cit.*, 221–223.
[27] Birrell, "Changes in Equity Procedure and Principles," in *A Century of Law Reform*, 177, 182 (1901).

common law did not attempt, and therein lies the great distinction between law and equity pleading. The process of "scraping the defendant's conscience," as it was called, by successive amendments of the bill which he had to answer until the plaintiff finally got all the admissions possible, was not permitted to go beyond the defendant's oath. He could not cross-examine him; and if the defendant were willing to lie, the plaintiff would lose, unless he had other witnesses to prove his case, because the church forsooth was unwilling to permit a defendant to win a law suit at the price of his soul! It was not until 1843 that a plaintiff was permitted to examine a defendant as a witness.[28]

The method of taking testimony in Chancery was even more absurd than equity pleading. Until 1852 testimony was taken by depositions on interrogatories in secret before examiners in the absence of counsel. Imagine the futility of attempting to cross-examine a witness on interrogatories without knowing his direct testimony or even the interrogatories put to him by the other side. Imagine the impossibility of dealing with hostile witnesses. After the taking of testimony before the examiners had at long last been completed came the interminable task of getting on to a hearing and, after the hearing, of getting a decision. Let Charles Dickens, who according to Holdsworth [29] has told the truth about *Jarndyce and Jarndyce* in *Bleak House,* pronounce judgment:

[28] 6 and 7 Vict. c. 85, sec. 1.
[29] Holdsworth, *Charles Dickens as a Legal Historian,* 1 (1929).

"This is the Court of Chancery which has its decaying houses and its blighted lands in every shire, which has its worn-out lunatic in every madhouse and its dead in every churchyard, which has its ruined suitor, with his slipshod heels and threadbare dress, borrowing and begging through the round of every man's acquaintance; which gives to monied might the means abundantly of wearying out the right; which so exhausts finances, patience, courage, hope; so overthrows the brain and breaks the heart that there is not an honourable man among its practitioners who would not give—who does not often give—the warning, 'Suffer any wrong that can be done you rather than come here.' "

Dickens did not confine his attentions to the Court of Chancery. He paid his respects to the law courts in the *Pickwick Papers,* which immortalized the suit of *Bardell v. Pickwick.* Elsewhere he deals with the ecclesiastical courts and Doctors' Commons, not to mention the personalities of the law from the beadle, the constable, and the justice of the peace to the judges, barristers, and solicitors. The novels of Dickens did much to arouse the English people to the necessity for court reform. They touched the hearts of millions who knew nothing of the invective of Bentham, "the great questioner of things established," and his followers, the pamphleteers and the writers in the reviews. Collectively, under the leadership of a few courageous judges and lawyers, they forced the reorganization of the courts, the simplification of the judicial structure in the Judicature Acts (1873–1875) and the adoption of a simple, rational procedure based on rules of court having for their prime purpose the achievement of justice. These rules of court followed the essential principles of the Code of Civil Procedure of David Dudley Field. Although the fundamentals of judicial reform have been achieved in England, the English bench and bar have continued to have their grave procedural problems. The recent report of the Evershed Committee,[30] so called in honor of its distinguished chairman, the Master of the Rolls, discusses many matters most of which revolve around the ancient division of the legal profession into barristers and solicitors and the vexing problem of costs. The seriousness of the situation is described by L. C. B. Gower: "If English procedure is the best, it is equally among the most expensive, and its expense is speedily making it a luxury beyond the reach of most individuals. Until recently only the dwindling number of the rich could contemplate litigation with equanimity; now, thanks to the Legal Aid Scheme, the dwindling number of the poor with disposable income of under £420 can face it with even greater nonchalance, but to those in the growing 'middle income brackets' it remains unattainable." [31]

The problem of costs remains the one dark blot on the British system of justice. The loss of a single law suit may spell financial ruin; thus the costs assessed against

[30] Cmd. 8878 (1953).
[31] 17 *Modern L. Rev.* 1 (1954).

the loser in *Graigola Merthyr Ltd. v. Swansea Corp.* in a trial lasting sixty days came to £77,000.[32] On the other hand, the English may point with pride to the fact that their barristers have given England an unrivalled brand of advocacy and from their midst has been selected a corps of judges who have the complete confidence of the English people.

In this country the primary concern of the post-revolutionary period was with the adaptation of the substantive law to the needs of a new nation. Coupled with this was the struggle for the preservation of the principles of the common law against the attacks of the Jeffersonians, who favored all things French including the principles of the civil law. As might well be imagined, early Americans had little liking for the subtleties of the English procedure of that day. The English Court of Chancery, moreover, was anathema in several of the new states. But instead of attempting to simplify procedure and to make it useful in the search for truth, the equalitarian movement took another turn, the disastrous effects of which we still feel today. Lowering standards of admission to the bar and setting up a judiciary elected on political slates generally for short terms were, as we have seen, bad enough; but the most unfortunate result of the equalitarian assumption came in the actual trial of cases, for was not each lawyer in a case the equal of the judge, and each juror, too, the judge's equal? At common law the judge conducted the trial. His common

[32] As noted by Lord Chorley in *David Dudley Field Centenary Essays* 115 (1949).

law powers have been excellently summarized by Judge Merrill E. Otis:

"First—the power to state the really controverted issues. Second—the power to remove from the jury's consideration false issues that accidentally have crept in or purposely have been injected. Third—the power fairly to sum up and arrange the testimony offered. These are essential elements of the power. To do these things effectively they must be done orally, with freedom of repetition, freedom of illustration, and after arguments of counsel, so that the enlightenment they will give will not be utterly eclipsed.

"The fourth element in the power, expression of opinion by the judge as to how some issue of fact should be resolved, as to the credibility of witnesses, in actual practice is an element seldom used; it is a power reserved for that rare case when outrageous pettifoggery requires an immediate corrective, convincing and complete. Mere knowledge of the existence of that power oft-times nips pettifoggery in the tender bud." [33]

But as a result of the equalitarian movement of a century ago even to this day in 20 states the trial judge is prohibited from summing up the evidence; [34] in 36

[33] Otis, "The Judge to the Jury," 16 *Kans. City L. Rev.* 1, 14–15 (1937).

[34] Vanderbilt, ed., *Minimum Standards of Judicial Administration,* 226 (1949).

states from commenting on the evidence; [35] in 20 states in charging the jury in civil matters and in 18 states in criminal matters the charge of the judge to the jury precedes the summation of counsel.[36] Somehow the jury is expected to remember the trial court's charge after it has been subjected to the barrage and counter-barrage of oratory from counsel in the case. In two states the trial judge must instruct the jury in criminal cases that they are the judges not only of the facts but of the law! [37] In those states where these heresies persist one can best understand their adverse effects by comparing trials in the federal courts with those in the state courts.[38] It is folly for a state to avail itself of modern procedure and modern rules of evidence and still cling to these absurdities of the era of antiprofessionalism.

The great name in the history of reform in American procedure is David Dudley Field. A man of genius in a family of geniuses,[39] he was, as Pound puts it, "an examplar of the faith in conscious creative law-making which we have come to accept." [40] Discarding entirely the procedural blunders of the past, he swept aside fictions, technicalities, and foreign verbiage and constructed a new code of procedure based on the complete

[35] *ibid.*, 229.

[36] *ibid.*, 233.

[37] Howe, "Juries as Judges of Criminal Law," 52 *Harv. L. Rev.* 582, 614 (1939).

[38] Otis, *op. cit.*, 35.

[39] Rogers, *American Bar Leaders*, 50–51 (1932).

[40] Pound, "David Dudley Field: An Appraisal," in *David Dudley Field Centenary Essays* (1949).

abolition of the distinction between all forms of common-law actions and between actions at law and suits in equity, and he did this without changing substantive rights, duties, and liberties or remedies or remedial rights. In short, all procedural distinctions up to judgment were eliminated, and the purpose of the judgment when obtained was to protect some substantive right or enforce some primary duty. The judgment was always to be based on facts, which might consist of acts or omissions, and a statement of such basic facts was therefore essential in his view, for the remedy flows from the issuable facts.[41]

Field's original Code of Procedure was adopted in New York in 1848 and spread westward rapidly, finding acceptance in whole or in part in thirty states. It also furnished an example to the law reformers of England, although they wisely proceeded by flexible rules of court rather than by legislative code. Unfortunately the code was manhandled in New York and several other states by hostile judges and by amending legislatures, eventually becoming so overburdened with exceptions and provisos as to lose its original virtue and become a legal nightmare. Its original 391 sections grew by 1880 to over 3,400 sections. Such overamendment seems to be an inherent infirmity of legislative activity in prescribing procedure, and has led to the modern trend toward the English plan of controlling procedure by rules of court. Nevertheless, though Field's Code was perverted in many states, his monumental labors were not in vain,

[41] Pomeroy, *Code Remedies*, 5th ed., chap. I (1929).

for his basic ideas are still the foundation of the best modern procedure as typified by the Federal Rules of Civil Procedure.

The story of the struggle for the Federal Rules is an interesting one. I have heard it said by lawyers who knew him that Thomas W. Shelton did not know how to draw a writ of dower, but that is unimportant in view of his work as chairman of the Committee on Uniform Judicial Procedure of the American Bar Association appointed in 1912.[42] For nearly twenty years with untiring energy he led a crusade for an act to give the United States Supreme Court the same rule-making power in actions at law that it had long exercised in equity, and thus to avoid the evils of the Conformity Act, only to face the adamant opposition of Senator Thomas A. Walsh, then chairman of the Senate Judiciary Committee. Shelton's successor as committee chairman in 1930 reported to the American Bar Association his pessimism as to the possibilities of ever obtaining such legislation. Two years later his successor, a federal district judge, reported his personal opinion that the rule-making power was undesirable, and the following year the committee was discontinued on his recommendation. But in 1934 the same bill, sponsored this time by Attorney General Homer S. Cummings, became law.

The United States Supreme Court promptly appointed an Advisory Committee on Federal Rules of Civil Procedure under the leadership of former Attor-

[42] Cf. Annual Reports to American Bar Association of the Committee on Uniform Judicial Procedure from 1913 to 1930.

ney General William D. Mitchell, with Dean, now Judge, Charles E. Clark as reporter. The committee was authorized to prepare rules of procedure abolishing the separation of law and equity in the federal courts.[43] The committee deserves as much credit for its methods of work as for the rules that it drafted. It solicited suggestions from individual judges and lawyers and from committees organized by every city, state, and federal bar association. Thus the committee had at its disposal and sought to utilize the best practice of the several states and likewise to profit from English experience. Tentative drafts of proposed rules were successively submitted for the criticism of these cooperating committees and of the bench and bar of the country generally, so that the final draft of the Federal Rules of Civil Procedure may be said to embody the experience not only of an unusually able committee but of the legal profession throughout the entire country. This method of operation has become standard for later committees, both federal and state, which have undertaken similar responsibilities. The rules themselves, which were promulgated in 1937, effective in 1938, are a model of simplicity and flexibility. They have already been made the basis of reform in several states [44] and it may safely be said that their influence in the states will be lasting, for in 1947 the Advisory Committee, having been continued by the Supreme Court, submitted amendments

[43] 295 U.S. 774 (1935).
[44] Vanderbilt, ed., *op. cit.*, 142; Barron and Holtzoff, *Federal Practice and Procedure* 1, 69. (1950 and 1954 pocket part).

to 32 of the 86 original rules, all of which became effective on March 19, 1948, and within the past five months it has submitted 23 amendments which have yet to be acted on. It is clearly recognized that the rule-making process is a continuous one. In New Jersey it resulted in so many amendments suggested from time to time by judges and lawyers that at the end of five years a complete revision was clearly needed. I believe that any adequate use of the rule-making power will necessitate such revisions periodically.

In the individual states it is possible to employ in the rule-making process a device not available in the federal system by reason of the size of the country. I refer to the use of what we in New Jersey call our judicial conference. The conference is composed of all the judges in the state (except the magistrates), representatives of the Legislature, the attorney general, the county prosecutors, the deans of the law schools, the officers and trustees of the state bar association, the presidents of the county bar associations, sixty lawyers appointed by the county bar presidents, and ten laymen appointed by the chief justice. It meets regularly once a year and occasionally in special sessions to discuss the various recommendations for changes in rules or statutes that have been suggested by judges and lawyers. The ideas developed at such meetings have been of invaluable aid to the Supreme Court in the exercise of the rule-making power. Special topics are frequently assigned to temporary committees of experts for investigation, and their reports become subjects of general discussion in the conference. Not only does the Supreme Court benefit from the deliberations of a carefully selected body, but each member helps the work of administering the courts by conveying back to his home county the gist of the thinking of the conference. There is also a municipal magistrates conference which has rendered invaluable service in changing that body of judges from a miscellaneous assortment of former justices of the peace, recorders, and police judges to a corps of magistrates whose boast it is that in their state at least the 'fixing' of traffic tickets has become a lost art.

Turning from the method of preparing the Federal Rules of Civil Procedure to their substance, we note in particular two principles of fundamental importance. Rule 1 is the expression of their purpose: "They shall be construed to secure the just, speedy, and inexpensive determination of every action." This thought is amplified in Rule 2 of the Federal Rules of Criminal Procedure: "These rules are intended to provide for the just determination of every criminal proceeding. They shall be construed to secure simplicity in procedure, fairness in administration and the elimination of unjustifiable expense and delay." New Jersey, drawing on a rule first adopted in its court of last resort in 1845 and extended to its law courts in 1912, expresses the spirit of the new procedure even better it seems to me:

"The rules applicable to any court shall be considered as general rules for the government of the court and the conducting of causes; and as the design of them is to facilitate business and advance justice, they may be relaxed or dispensed with by the court in any cases where it shall be manifest to the court that a strict adherence to them will work surprise or injustice." [45]

Although this rule has been in force for many years, I have yet to hear of a case where it has been abused, and if any abuse ever should occur an appeal on the ground of abuse of discretion would speedily cure it. However phrased, the new procedure by rules of court is designed to promote justice, and rules of procedure are regarded merely as means to that end.

The second principle of our modern rules of procedure is closely related to the first; it involves the free use of all the available forms of pretrial procedures such as interrogatories, depositions, inspections, and examinations to enable each party to prepare his case fully for trial and thus to prevent surprise. Only with the elimination of surprise and technicalities can we hope to put an end to the sporting theory of justice. There is, of course, always the danger that the sound procedures designed to aid a party in preparation for trial may be abused, especially demands for interrogatories and the taking of depositions in discovery. Particularly has complaint been made in some quarters of the excessive taking of depositions in the federal courts. The matter, however, is entirely within the control of the trial judge, who must be as zealous to prevent such abuse as coun-

[45] Hartshorne, *The New Jersey Practice Act (1912) and Rules*, p. 28, Rule 5, taken from Rule 36 of Court of Errors and Appeals (1855), Soney & Sage, 1912.

sel should be to report it to him. Nothing could be more unfortunate for the orderly search for truth in the interest of justice than a curtailment of the legitimate use of the various pretrial procedures, and this is bound to occur if they are misused generally.

The chief controversy over the Federal Rules of Civil Procedure has been with respect to what constitutes a sufficient complaint or answer. One side asserts that the courts are occasionally giving judgment without any definite statement of claims for relief or of defense to justify it; the other claims that those who oppose this would restore the ancient forms of action, which Heaven forbid! The difficulty is not peculiar to this country. To avoid controversies at home let me quote an English case that deals with the problem succinctly and realistically. In *Banbury v. The Bank of Montreal* Lord Parker said:

"The trial judge is said to have misdirected—I think in several respects he did misdirect—the jury, but I cannot think he received the assistance which might have been expected in so complicated a case. . . . Nor do I blame counsel. The fault lies in the system which permits a plaintiff to set up at the trial without amending his pleadings a case other than that put forward in the statement of claim. When this is done the new case cannot possibly be formulated with the precision necessary to elucidate either the principles of law which may be applicable or the issues of fact which may be involved. Both the counsel and the

Judge labour under great disadvantages and a miscarriage of justice is all too likely to occur.

"The system of pleading introduced by the Judicature Acts was no doubt intended as a compromise between the rigid system which prevailed in the Common Law Courts and the loose prolixity of the Bill in Chancery. The Bill stated all the facts at great length and prayed such relief as the petitioner might be entitled to in the premises. The Chancellor or Vice-Chancellor had to find out for himself what might be the equities between the parties. For this he could take what time he liked and often took a very long time. The present practice appears to me to have most of the vices of the old procedure in Chancery. There are pleadings it is true, but the pleadings are for all practical purposes disregarded. The plaintiff is allowed to prove what he likes and set up any case he can. The Judge has no longer to deal with the case formulated on the pleading, but to make up his mind whether on the facts proved there is any, and what, case at all.

"The disadvantage is accentuated when there is a jury; the Judge cannot take time to consider the matter and counsel have not considered it as they would have done had they been compelled to embody their case in a statement of claim. Under these circumstances there is little wonder that a Judge should misdirect a jury and that the real question of law or fact should, as in this case, emerge only after a long discussion on appeal.

"Had the plaintiff, after admitting that it was not within the scope of the Bank's business to advise on Canadian investments at large, been compelled to amend his statement of claim by stating the special circumstances which, as he alleged, brought it within the scope of the Bank's business to advise the plaintiff on this particular investment, I doubt whether the action would have proceeded further, and I am clearly of opinion that the question of authority would not have been left to the jury. The impossibility of the plaintiff's case would have been manifest on the record." [46]

Perhaps in avoiding the one extreme of special pleading we have occasionally veered too far to the other extreme of unintelligible vagueness. In any event it does not seem too much to expect that at some time before trial the plaintiff should state, however informally, what makes him think he has a right to seek relief, and similarly the defendant should state, however informally, what makes him think he has a defense. In these days of liberal amendments such a simple requirement imposes no hardship on either party. The plaintiff and the defendant equally should not be permitted to mislead each other with respect to what they are seeking in court; there is no more justice in surprise in pleadings than there is in surprise with respect to evidence.

All difficulties with respect to the character of the pleadings may be fully resolved without engaging in

[46] [1918] A.C. at p. 709–710.

controversy as to the nature of pleadings by resort in every case to a thoroughgoing pretrial conference, a device for improving trials in the interest of justice, for shortening them and incidentally for promoting settlements as each side learns for the first time of the strength of his adversary's case and the weakness of his own. The pretrial conference results, as we shall see, in an order which supersedes the pleadings, and incidentally all controversies as to the nature of pleadings. In effect, the pretrial conference order constitutes the directions that "controls the subsequent course of action [in the litigation] unless modified at or before the trial . . . to prevent manifest injustice." [47]

Of all the pretrial devices the pretrial conference is by all odds the most important. I gather from what I read in the newspapers that some judges in other states conceive of a pretrial conference solely as a means of forcing settlements. There could be no greater mistake and no conduct better devised to bring the administration of justice into disrepute. We have found, to be sure, that largely as a result of the pretrial conferences three cases out of four are customarily settled after both parties have had to face for the first time the facts on each side under expert guidance, but in our state settlements are not forced and counsel would not hesitate to complain if force were attempted. With us settlements, when they come, are a mere incident of the pretrial conferences, resulting from the new view that counsel and the litigants have of their case after the pretrial confer-

[47] N.J. Rules of Court 4:29–1 (1953).

ence. Nor do we regard it as a primary consideration that as a result of pretrial conferences the cases that do go on to trial are disposed of in from a third to a half less time than when there was no pretrial conference in our state. No, the grand objective of a pretrial conference is to prepare the trial judge and counsel on each side for the best possible trial of such cases as are fought to a conclusion.

At the pretrial conference first the plaintiff and then the defendant state what each expects to prove at the trial. The trial judge thereupon dictates for the pretrial order the issues to be proved and if any amendments of the pleadings are necessary he orders them made. Next the court explores what facts may be admitted. Thus if there is no controversy in an automobile negligence case as to the defendant's ownership of the car or of his son's agency to operate it, those essential facts are admitted in the pretrial order. If the suit mainly concerns the plaintiff's personal injuries and the damages to his car are relatively slight, the court will seek to get the parties to agree as to the amount of damages to the plaintiff's car, thus avoiding calling witnesses on a minor issue. If there are documents which will be necessary at the trial and their execution and admissibility is uncontroverted, they will be marked in evidence immediately thus saving the time of taking the formal proof of attesting witnesses. All of these matters will be incorporated in the pretrial order, which is dictated in open court and signed on the spot by both court and counsel. I stress the importance of this work being done in open court rather than in the judge's chambers as so many judges seem to prefer, first, because it is the most important step in the case, second, because it is difficult judicial work and cannot be done well in the leisurely informality of the judge's chambers, and finally, because the clients are entitled to and should be present to aid their counsel with respect to the facts. Such a conference is an indispensable preliminary to the best possible kind of trial. Among other things, it gives the trial judge an opportunity to order the preparation of briefs to be delivered in advance of trial, if he thinks such briefs are necessary. No longer does the trial judge have to fumble through the pleadings at the trial to find out what the case is all about while endeavoring to listen to the opening statements of counsel. No longer does he find it necessary to retire to chambers to prepare his charge to the jury during the closing arguments of counsel, thus leaving the courtroom without a presiding officer. He has before him in a pretrial conference order a complete outline of the course that the trial will take; he is the master of the situation from the outset to the conclusion of the trial.

I will not pretend that the acceptance of mandatory pretrial conferences came easily in New Jersey. The trial lawyers did not like the idea of giving up the techniques they had studied and used for years, but they were reluctantly persuaded to try the new system tentatively, because their intelligence told them not only that it meant a better brand of justice but that they could dispose of many more cases a month under the new system than they could under the old regime. They were impressed by what they saw at a demonstration staged for us by some of the leading lawyers of Washington, D.C., under the direction of Chief Judge Bolitha J. Laws. Many of the judges of our law courts, however, saw nothing good in it, and it required the utmost in persuasion in some instances to get them to give the matter the effort which it requires, for directing a good pretrial conference in a complicated case is no mean intellectual feat. It took a year or two to begin to obtain the desired results from many of the judges, and new judges require instruction in the art in addition to the information contained in the pretrial conference manual prepared for the use of the bench and the bar.[48]

After the trial attorneys and the trial judges had been won over, another difficulty revealed itself; the casualty companies were sending to the pretrial conferences young branch office attorneys who knew little about the facts of the case and still less about how to try it and with no authority to make admissions. We then asked the representatives of the casualty companies to change their practice and to send each summons and complaint to trial counsel immediately after its receipt by the company so that trial counsel might come to the pretrial conference fully informed about the case and duly authorized to make the necessary admissions for the preparation of an adequate pretrial conference order. We were told that to do this would cost the companies well over $1,000,000 a year in increased lawyers' fees in New Jersey alone. We countered by asking how many

[48] N.J. Manual of Pretrial Practice (1953).

million dollars the companies were saving by being able to take down their reserves against pending cases within six months instead of the traditional two and a half to three years. When the matter was presented from this angle, the companies quickly agreed to cooperate as long as we kept our docket current, because they were saving several times the million dollars involved in additional lawyers' fees. I need not add that this arrangement was entirely satisfactory to our trial bar.

Much as the Federal Rules of Civil Procedure had been needed, there was an even greater necessity for the reform of criminal procedure. Due to the outstanding example of the Federal Rules of Civil Procedure and the favorable attitude of Attorney General Jackson, the victory for the reform of criminal procedure was as swift as the struggle for reform of civil procedure had been prolonged and difficult. The bill [49] recommended by the Section of Criminal Law of the American Bar Association authorizing the Supreme Court to act was passed within a year of its submission to Congress, and in February, 1941, the Supreme Court appointed an Advisory Committee. Several drafts were prepared and distributed in the same manner as in the case of the Civil Rules, and these received the careful attention of lawyers everywhere. Many of the Criminal Rules involved difficult constitutional questions as well as a careful balancing of the public interest and private rights. The rules in final form were promulgated by the Supreme Court on December 26, 1944, and though the Judiciary

[49] Act of June 29, 1940, c. 445, 54 Stat. 688; 18 U.S.C. sec. 687.

Committees of the Congress had the power, as with the Civil Rules, to hold hearings and consider the Criminal Rules, they did not do so.

There is one interesting incident in connection with the Criminal Rules that deserves recounting here because it illustrates how continuous is the struggle for a fair trial. Among the rules recommended to the Supreme Court by its Advisory Committee was one aimed at the elimination of the practice, prevailing in certain districts of the government, of submitting a so-called "confidential brief" to the trial court without furnishing the defendant or his counsel with a copy. Often these briefs went far beyond a statement of the government's view of the law of the case and detailed the evidence the government hoped to elicit from its witnesses. The unfairness of this practice is obvious, yet for some reason not disclosed to the Advisory Committee the Supreme Court deleted the proposed rule. Months later one of the Justices told me that the Court did so because it felt that the rule was an affront to the dignity of the trial judges (!), though the rule was in fact directed to attorneys and not to the trial courts. The matter, however, did not end there, for some of the federal judges continued their opposition to the practice with the result that we find recorded in the Report of the Annual Conference of Senior Circuit Judges held in October, 1946, a minute reading: "The Conference, after consideration of the report of the Committee appointed to study the subject matter, disapproved the practice, prevalent in some districts, of trial judges in criminal cases receiving from the attorney on one side a brief or trial memorandum that has not been furnished to the attorney on the other side, and recommended the immediate discontinuance of such practice." [50]

Another battle for the right to a fair trial had been won. So far as I know, this was the first time that the senior circuit judges with the aid of the Chief Justice in effect overruled the Supreme Court, but of the soundness of their decision there can be no doubt. The incident is also significant as an example of the difference between law in the books and law in action. A study merely of the history of the Federal Rules of Criminal Procedure would show the recommendation to the Supreme Court by its Advisory Committee of a rule against the submission of confidential briefs by attorneys and the Court's rejection of the proposed rule. From the books alone therefore the argument might be made that the Supreme Court still approved of confidential briefs. Yet the action taken by the Annual Conference in 1946, without amending the rules, did away with a bad practice by administrative action.

Improvements are likewise being made in appellate procedure and administration. We have gone far since the day when a proceeding to review a judgment was treated as a new suit with a separate writ and pleadings. No longer is it necessary to reduce the testimony in an equity suit to narrative form at the cost of many hours of useless labor. For no rule of court have I ever voted

[50] Report of the Judicial Conference of Senior Circuit Judges (1946), p. 21.

with more pleasure than for the simple one which read, "Assignments of error, bills of exceptions, grounds of appeal, petitions of appeal, specifications of causes for reversal, and writs of error are abolished." How many hours of wasted labor these phrases connote! Now all one needs to do in progressive states is to serve his adversary with a simple notice of appeal and file it with the court. The headings of his brief will indicate what his grounds of appeal are—and indicate them in their finished form, which was something the earlier lengthy appellate pleadings filed soon after the trial never did. At that time counsel's main object was to catch and save every possible ground of appeal, many of which on reflection he had to abandon.

In a few states even greater progress in appellate matters is to be found in matters of administration, though regrettably in many states the briefs are not read in advance of the oral argument; indeed in a considerable number of states there is little oral argument, cases being submitted merely on briefs in many instances. I can conceive of nothing in the whole field of procedure quite as futile as an appellate court solemnly listening to the argument of counsel without having read and analyzed the briefs that counsel have gone—or should have gone—to great pains to prepare. Every member of the court should read the briefs and as much of the record as he is referred to in the briefs in advance of oral argument, he should prepare a typewritten memorandum of his tentative views, and it is also very helpful for the judges to indicate to the presiding judge in advance

which points they would like to hear argued most extensively, so that he may advise counsel at the outset of
their argument which points most interest or concern the
court, leaving it to counsel, of course, to employ their
time as they see fit. After hearing the arguments of
counsel and particularly after listening to their answers
to any questions which have been troubling us, we often
find ourselves changing the views we had tentatively
reached after the reading of the briefs. If this is so, I am
sometimes asked, why read the briefs and record before
the argument? There are several reasons: If you prepare yourself in advance, you will know what questions
the briefs leave unanswered and you can ask these questions at the oral argument. If you read the briefs and
record only after the argument, counsel will not be
available to answer the questions you would like to ask.
Advance preparation, moreover, saves the court from
asking questions it would not have to ask if it had read
the briefs. Arguments to an enlightened court move
faster than arguments to an uninformed court. Furthermore, if counsel know that the court is familiar with the
case, the temptation to shade the facts or to color the
law is removed; the penalty of exposure at the oral argument is something most counsel do not wish to endure.
Finally, the volume of case law in each state is so vast
that no judge can possibly know all the decisions; it is
a great advantage to the judges therefore to get a general view of the law of the case before listening to the
several parts of the argument.

Not only does sound judicial administration require

the study of the briefs in advance of the oral argument, but it demands that the decision of the appeal follow promptly after the argument. I have never been able to understand how our judges in New Jersey under the old system could be expected to hear arguments day after day for two weeks and really remember what counsel had said in every case, especially as they had not read the briefs and record in advance. Frankly, I know that I could not and perhaps I may be pardoned for doubting whether many other judges can do it. Even if I could, I should not think it worth while to make the mental effort when a more rational method is available. The English practice is infinitely preferable, in so far as it permits the judges to concentrate upon one case and dispose of it before proceeding to the next. There each case is argued at length, often for days, and it is generally decided before going on to the next case. I heard the conclusion of an argument in the Privy Council that lasted a week. I asked the clerk when it would be decided. He said, "This afternoon, and one of the judges will write the opinion over the weekend and you may read it in The Times next Tuesday." And I did! That system is, of course, impossible in this country, but in New Jersey we hear arguments on Mondays in five or six appeals. Then we adjourn until Thursday to give us a chance to restudy the briefs in the light of the oral arguments. During the week we also study motions and petitions for certification which are submitted on briefs alone. On Thursday, after each justice has expressed his views at length, a tentative vote is taken and the case is assigned for the writing of an opinion.

There is a great deal of mystery as to how some appellate courts work, and a great deal of this mystery, I fear, would not stand the light of day. In more than half of the appellate courts in the several states opinions are assigned in rotation in advance of the oral argument. Judges, being mere men, doubtless listen more attentively to the arguments in the case where they are to write the opinion than they do to the arguments in other cases. There is an art, I am told, of seeming to listen. In some jurisdictions the practice of rotation has been exalted to a cardinal principle; judges have been called upon to write an opinion for the majority of the court with which they did not agree, but then they have been permitted to accompany such a majority opinion with a dissenting opinion of their own expressing their true views! There are other courts in which there is no conference at all after the argument, but the judge to whom the case is assigned in rotation writes an opinion which is circulated and if nobody dissents, it becomes the opinion of the court without any conference whatsoever. If the judge disagrees with the opinion writer, he may prepare a dissenting opinion and circularize it, but a mere description of this process discloses its weakness. No opinion, I submit, should become the opinion of the court without a full discussion by the entire court of all the issues developed at the argument before the case is assigned for the writing of the opinion; and after the opinion has been written, it should likewise be studied by every member of the court and subjected to frank criticism in conference both as to substance and language. One-judge opinions are really a fraud on the litigants and the public.

To summarize, in most of our states we have come a long way from the old common-law procedure of technicalities and fictions, though these arch enemies of decisions on the merits of a case are by no means dead in this country. Modern procedure is now available that is simple, flexible, and adapted to the needs of the individual case at both the trial and appellate levels, but it is yet to be accepted in most jurisdictions. No state has yet made the progress in the matter of rules of evidence that some have made in procedure and pleading. Now the Uniform Rules of Evidence provide the means for moving forward. Finally, even in those jurisdictions where improved procedure has been adopted, experience has taught us that continual revision will always be necessary if our procedure is to be kept free from defects that are made apparent by actual courtroom experience. Even in the jurisdictions that are committed to continuous revision we must cease to be parochial and dedicate ourselves to a comparative study of procedure in action in every system of law. We must know what is being done not only in other American states, for there is much that we may learn from each other, but we must also go beyond the common-law jurisdictions and familiarize ourselves with the procedure of other civilized countries governed by the civil law. We must evaluate all we learn elsewhere fairly and be prepared to adopt it if it is better than what we now have.

This is a great task that cannot be accomplished by a few judges or practicing lawyers. It can only be done in the law schools and it can be done best on a cooperative basis; I shall say more on this point in my final chapter. Only by so doing may we hope to produce a superior kind of justice in action. The task will be an onerous one, but who can doubt that if we achieve it, men will gladly turn from such makeshift devices as commercial arbitration and administrative agencies manned largely by laymen and look to the courts when they are seeking the vindication of their rights?

CHAPTER IV

Effective Administration
and Less Delay

OF the popular complaints about the courts the one most frequently heard is that directed to the law's delays. The law's delays constitute a problem, or rather a series of problems, that are best discussed quite apart from the elimination of technicalities and surprise; a state may have a simple, flexible system of procedure and still be vexed by unnecessary delays, though, needless to say, cumbersome procedure will inevitably add to the inefficiency of its courts. Fortunately the law's delays are a curable disease, if judges and lawyers can only be induced to change their working habits to conform to practices in line with those obtaining in the business world. In so doing not only will they obviate a great cause of popular complaint, but they will improve both the quality of their work and the amount of their output, and incidentally render their labors far less arduous than they now are. These statements may seem extravagant, but I can demonstrate their accuracy from personal experience in New Jersey over the past six years.

But first I should like to make some preliminary observations with respect to the popular complaints directed at the law's delays; next I should like to show

how chronic this disease is at least in our large cities—unfortunately there are no statistics available to show whether or not it is equally true in the smaller communities—and then I shall sketch the situation that prevailed in New Jersey in 1948 and the several steps by which court congestion there was eliminated and public respect for the law and judges and lawyers immeasurably increased. After that I should like also to describe the work of the Administrative Office of the Courts in New Jersey, without which we could not have overcome the law's delays, and finally I should like to outline the work of the Administrative Office of the United States Courts, because as the first such office to be established it has set the pattern for such administrative work on a national scale.

In considering the work of the courts we must constantly keep in mind that in almost every law suit there is at least one party, generally the defendant, who is wholeheartedly in favor of the law's delays. Thus for this and other reasons, as we shall see, the blame for delay does not rest altogether on the courts. They must be given the power and the judicial machinery to make sure that litigants who desire delay are unsuccessful in their efforts. They should not have any more time to prepare their case than is reasonable. Here, too, we encounter the perennial tendency of the legal profession to procrastinate, and the perfectly human desire of members of a profession to accommodate each other. It is essential that the court have both the power to keep these matters under control and the machinery to reveal whether or not a given case is proceeding according to the schedule prescribed.

Every case, moreover, inevitably takes time for the preparation of an answer, sometimes for motions addressed to the pleadings, and regularly for pretrial procedures such as inspections, interrogatories, and depositions, which should culminate, except in criminal and matrimonial cases, in a pretrial conference. Time also must be allowed for a waiting period of at least two weeks after the pretrial conference before the case goes on the daily trial calendar. During this waiting period the parties, who, as we have seen, now really know their case for the first time, may meditate the desirability of settlement and act on it before running the risk of trial. Generally speaking, any attempt without the consent of the parties to shorten the time for any of these steps in preparation for trial—a period of almost five months in an ordinary case—is likely to result in a miscarriage of justice. It is therefore obvious that the emphasis from the court's point of view should be placed, first, on a well-prepared case, second, on the elimination of any waiting time after a case has been properly prepared and is awaiting trial and, finally, on obtaining a prompt decision after trial and a prompt review on appeal, if desired. I shall discuss each of these matters in detail.

Nor must we ever forget that every law suit is unique, at least it is so regarded by its participants, who rightly believe that they are entitled to the best possible kind of justice at the hands of the court and jury consistent with common sense in a workaday world. If this be so—and there is no gainsaying it—mass production methods and assembly line techniques are utterly incompatible with the sound administration of justice. Every case is entitled to all the time and individual attention necessary for a fair trial considering all the circumstances of the case, but not to one minute for delaying tactics.

If we had to decide between justice administered as rapidly as possible consistent with the allowance of a fair amount of time for preparation for trial in the manner just outlined and a possible better brand of justice to be obtained by taking a longer time, I would unhesitatingly favor the better, slower kind of justice. But the kind of justice I have been discussing contemplates the full discovery of facts before trial and thorough preparation on the law by counsel. Any further allowance of time would result not in a better but in a lesser kind of justice, since it would be an unreasonably delayed justice. With those objectives in mind, a trial becomes not a sporting event, as Dean Wigmore has aptly characterized the old practice, but an orderly search for truth in the interests of justice. With pretrial procedures to get at the facts, with a pretrial conference to limit the trial to the real points in controversy, and with trial briefs, where necessary, made available to the court in advance of trial, there is no reason why in nonjury cases the trial judge, having studied the trial briefs and having heard the evidence and having listened to the closing arguments of counsel, should not be in a position to decide the case at once. He will never know more about it than he does at that time. The moment for decision has arrived, before other cases intervene to dull and blur his grasp of the pending case. How often have we known judges burdened with so many undecided matters that they were exhausting their intellectual effort in determining which case to dispose of first, and devoting what little strength they had left to telling all and sundry how overworked they were? Sound rules of administration requiring briefs in advance and prompt decisions after argument will spare them all these worries and their friends the burden of listening to their woes. I know someone will immediately suggest that the judge may wish to look up more law; the answer is he should have called for it earlier. All of us know that in most cases, both at the trial level and on appeals, it is the facts rather than the law that cause us most difficulty. If a judge cannot decide a motion within a week or a case within four weeks, he should frankly say so and call for a reargument to get himself off dead center and then start over. The farther the judge gets away from the trial and the more matters intervene, the more elusive will the facts and the "feel" of a given case become.

By such simple means as these, self-enforced by weekly reports, we have been able in New Jersey to overcome entirely the bad habit of reserved decisions. Once the new habit had been established, nobody would return to the old practice which brought so much disrespect on some of our courts and caused the judges so much unnecessary work.

Everyone who reads the newspapers should be familiar with the congestion of litigation in both the state and federal courts in most of our large cities, but what they do not realize, unless they have cause to investigate the matter, is that this congestion is chronic. It has been allowed to run on for decades, in some places for more than a century, while our judges and lawyers, who are professionally responsible for its cure, and our governors and legislators, a majority of whom are lawyers, sit idly by as if the disease were hopeless or they were not responsible. But most emphatically it may be said that the disease is curable, and if the members of the legal profession are not responsible for effecting its cure, who is? It is not to our credit that where cures have occurred, they have generally been effected under the impetus of a popular revolt of laymen against the quaint professional notion that the courts exist primarily for the benefit of judges and lawyers and only incidentally for the benefit of the litigants and the state.

According to figures gathered this year (1954) by the Institute of Judicial Administration, a jury case has to wait for trial 37 months in New York County, in Kings County 45 months, and in Queens County 49 months from the date of reaching issue.[1] Going back over a century, in 1839 we find David Dudley Field writing of the New York courts: "Speedy justice is a thing unknown; and any justice, without delays almost ruinous, is most rare." [2] Justification for his statement may be found in

[1] Institute of Judicial Administration, *State Trial Courts of General Jurisdiction, Calendar Status Study–1945*, June 30, 1954, p. 3.

[2] David Dudley Field, *Letter to Gulian C. Verplanck, on The Reform of the Judicial System of this State*, 8 (1840).

the *Democratic Review* for 1846, which pointed out that it would take two and a half years to dispose of the business then before the Supreme Court of New York City if no new cases were entrusted to it, that the Court of Errors was "Upward of two years in arrears . . . and will soon have three years of work undisposed of on its calendar . . . a party filing a bill today [in the Court of Chancery] would have no reason to expect a final decree in less than five years." [3]

In 1904, over half a century later, a distinguished Commission on the Law's Delays headed by Wheeler H. Peckham concluded its summary of the state of the court calendars in New York by observing: "The situation thus disclosed is of the gravest character." [4] But there has been virtually no improvement for over a century in the most populous state in the Union despite the fine work of twenty-five successive commissions and committees with reports aggregating over 30,000 pages and a judicial council now in its twentieth year.

Massachusetts cities are as far behind as New York. It takes 34 months for a ready case to be reached for trial in Suffok County (Boston) and 42 months in Worcester County, despite the reports of forty-one commissions and committees since 1851 and a judicial council now in its thirty-ninth year.[5] In Cook County, Illinois, 36 months is required, a condition of long standing

[3] Quoted in Nims, "New York's 100 Years Struggle for Better Civil Justice," 25 *N.Y. State Bar Bull.* 83 (1953).

[4] *ibid.*, 85.

[5] *op. cit.*, Inst. of Jud. Adm., p. 2.

despite the removal from the courts in 1913 of suits by workmen against employers.[6] A case in Hartford County, Connecticut, takes 31 months to be reached,[7] and in Allegheny County (Pittsburgh), Pennsylvania, 21 months.[8] This, indeed, is a sad commentary on American justice.

From our experience in New Jersey under our new Constitution I have no hesitation in saying that any jurisdiction that really wants to eliminate congested calendars may readily do so without resort to the un-judicial methods that have occasionally characterized similar efforts elsewhere, such as forcing settlements by putting a case at the bottom of the calendar if the parties will not settle. The bench and bar of New Jersey have traditionally been conservative and still are. We are one of the few states where the judges are appointed, not elected. We are one of the few states where the trial judge still retains all of his common-law powers. But for a variety of reasons that it is not necessary to discuss here, our courts had fallen into disfavor with the public. In 1947, over the opposition of all but a handful of judges and lawyers and without any support from a single bar association, the people adopted a new Constitution by a vote of three and a half to one, creating a streamlined judicial establishment.

Our former Court of Chancery had been notorious for its delays, not so much in getting cases to trial as in

[6] *ibid.*, 2.
[7] *ibid.*, 1.
[8] *ibid.*, 4.

deciding them after trial. Delays of two, three, and four years in handing down decisions were not uncommon, and delays of ten and twelve years were not unknown. Some of the vice chancellors resembled Lord Eldon, at least in his capacity for procrastination, and apparently they had never heard of Dickens' *Bleak House* and the famous case of *Jarndyce and Jarndyce* which I have mentioned before. The work of the ten vice chancellors under the old regime has now been taken over by six judges of the Chancery Division of the Superior Court, all of whom regularly decide motions within a week and cases within four weeks after trial as now required by the rules of court. The curse of undue delays in equity litigation has been eliminated by the application of simple rules of administration. Our judges under the inspiration of these new administrative rules have discovered that it is easier to decide a case than to invent a reason for not deciding it. Similarly seven matrimonial judges now accomplish with more satisfactory results the work formerly carried on by twelve matrimonial masters. It is significant that the judges responsible for the success of the new system are for the most part the same judges who had been on the bench under the old regime. What better proof can one ask of the value of sound rules of administration regularly complied with?

The problem of the congestion of cases awaiting trial was, of course, greatest in the law courts with their heavy load of negligence litigation. Many cases were over two years old; some ran back as much as thirteen years.[9] In the first year under the new system the Law Division of the Superior Court, with one judge less than its predecessor court under the old system, disposed of 93% more cases.[10] In the county courts, with the same number of judges as under the old system, the increase in the number of cases disposed of in the first year under the new Constitution was 82%.[11] As in chancery and matrimonial matters, the same judges were at work, again furnishing convincing proof of the value of sound administrative practices. In the second year the law courts increased their productivity by 19% over the first year.[12] Despite increases in the number of cases being started, at the end of the third year the number of cases on the calendar was the smallest in twenty years.[13] The problem of chronic calendar congestion had been solved in New Jersey, and at the same time the cases were by common consent being better tried than under the old system.

The results attained in New Jersey in eliminating undue delay in the administration of justice are attributable to several factors, each of which I believe to be indispensable to the desired result.

Our citizens are very conscious of the fact that it was

[9] Annual Report of the Administrative Director, 1948–49, p. 11.
[10] *ibid.*, 83.
[11] *ibid.*, 83.
[12] Annual Report of the Administrative Director, 1949–50, Summary A.
[13] Annual Report of the Administrative Director, 1950–51, Table G-2.

their struggle and not any program of the bench and bar generally that brought about judicial reform in the Constitution of 1947. Since then they have come to expect the best possible of their judges and lawyers and on more than one occasion have made it evident that they will tolerate nothing less. This popular sentiment is of immense value in overcoming the inertia that seems to be an almost inescapable characteristic of every branch of the legal profession. In building a sound judicial establishment the importance of this popular sentiment cannot be overestimated.

Almost as fundamental is the necessity for a simple system of courts. All that is really needed in a modern judicial establishment is a local court of limited civil and criminal jurisdiction, a trial court of general statewide jurisdiction, and an appellate court or courts, depending on the needs of the particular state. Often civil courts are differentiated from the criminal courts, but this is by no means necessary. Very few of our states have such a simple system, though why we need cling to the intricacies of jurisdiction that we inherited from England, accumulated in our growth from colonies to states, or acquired while our states were changing from an aggregation of small communities to complicated industrial areas, is difficult to say. The symmetry of the New Jersey system of courts was marred by the retention for political reasons of the county courts with jurisdiction largely the same as that of the Superior Court,[14] but

[14] Assembly Bill 36, 1953 Session, would have corrected this by transferring the jurisdiction of the County Courts to the Supe-

from an administrative standpoint this defect has been largely overcome through the power of the chief justice to assign county judges to sit temporarily in the Superior Court and Superior Court judges to sit in the county courts with the result that they all work on a common list.

Judicial work is of various kinds: appellate, criminal, civil, equity, probate, and matrimonial. A judge who is equally interested or equally proficient in all of them is indeed a rarity. Every judge, if he is to do his best work, should be assigned, wherever possible, to the kind of judicial business in which he excels. Some very good trial judges shudder at the thought of opinion writing. Some very good equity judges shrink from working with a jury. In the interest of sound judicial administration, therefore, someone should be authorized to assign the judges to the kind of work which they can best do. Because this power of assignment is a delicate one to be exercised only on mature reflection in the interest of the judicial establishment as a whole, it should be committed to the chief judicial officer of the state and he, in turn, would do well to seek the advice of his colleagues, even though the ultimate responsibility must be solely his.

It is equally important that judges be assigned to the places where there is judicial work for them to do. It is intolerably bad business administration to have some judges overworked while others sit by half idle as in

rior Court. It passed the Assembly 32 to 14 but died in Senate Committee.

some jurisdictions. This is especially so where the over-worked judges and the half idle judges are located in the same courthouse, as is often the situation where there is a complicated system of courts in which no one has the power to transfer judges from one court to another. Where for any reason an undue load of cases has accumulated, the number of judges assigned there must be increased either temporarily or permanently. Here a curious but nevertheless demonstrable judicial phenomenon comes into play. Two judges in the same courthouse working from a common calendar can dispose of half again as many cases as they can working on separate lists in different courthouses. The extent to which this principle may be applied is limited only by the number of available courtrooms, the number of available trial judges, and the number of available trial lawyers. Accordingly the increase in the number of judges at a congested spot, either permanently or temporarily, is the first step in bringing cases to a prompt trial. This means that someone must be given the power to assign the trial judges to those courts where they are most needed. Clearly the individual best equipped to do this is the chief justice, though here again he will do well to take the advice of his colleagues. It is a power that is also essential in meeting emergencies caused by illness, which is not uncommon among older men, or by some unusually long case which would otherwise hold up an entire calendar, or a failure to fill a judicial vacancy promptly.

Another factor that is rarely discussed in public but

which I can assure you is nevertheless much in the minds of the judges, is the principle of a fair division of work among them. Some judges are much more effective in their work than others; some are reversed less frequently than others; some judges give more satisfaction personally to the bar and the public; some are more diligent, more conscientious, more devoted to their work than others. These individual differences cannot be changed administratively, but equality in the time judges of the same court spend at their work of hearing cases should and can be achieved administratively. It irks the competent, conscientious judge to put in a full day on the bench each working day of the week, every week of the court year, when he knows that there are other judges who are finding excuses for failing to do so. This can easily be corrected by a rule of court prescribing the hours every judge shall sit (in our state five hours a day five days a week for law and matrimonial judges and four days a week for equity judges) [15] and by having each judge submit at the end of each week a report of his hours on the bench each court day with a list of the cases and motions he heard and a list of matters in which decision was reserved.[16] From these weekly reports summaries may be quickly prepared and

[15] Rule 1:28–2.

[16] Rule 1:30–2, Deciding of Motions and Cases, reads as follows: "As a matter of routine, all motions heard by the trial courts in any week shall be decided at or before the opening of the court the next week. As a matter of routine, all cases submitted to trial courts shall be decided within four weeks after submission."

distributed to all of the judges of each court. You may ask, how will this make an indolent judge work? The chief justice, of course, cannot hope to make a lazy judge work, nor is it to be expected that he will be a policeman, but when the weekly summaries are distributed to the judges in each court it is truly remarkable to see how the relatively few laggards respond to the prodding of their fellow judges. Very often such lapses were due to the fact that they believed that everyone else was likewise taking things easy. These weekly reports serve the valuable purpose also of revealing where calendar difficulties are being encountered, thus enabling the chief justice to make the necessary temporary assignments to take care of them and thus to prevent new inequalities from arising.

These weekly reports and other data supplied by the county clerks and prosecutors are compiled into a monthly report by the administrative director of the courts, and in due course are combined into quarterly and annual reports. These reports provide a wealth of information on the work of the individual judges and permit each of them and the public to compare his record with those of his colleagues. These "live" statistics, as we call them, are far more useful than the historical or "dead" statistics which are collected in some states, recording, as they do, merely what has happened a year or two before.

So much for problems of court organization and personnel. Equally important in effective judicial procedure are rules of court promulgated by the highest court of the state governing the procedure of *all* of the courts. Nothing is more disheartening to the bar than conflicting rules in various courts. These rules have as their paramount objectives the outmoding of procedural technicalities and the elimination of surprise,[17] those twin allies of the sporting theory of justice that are utterly inconsistent with the modern concept of a trial as a search for truth in the interest of justice. Surprise, as we have seen, can ordinarily be avoided by the liberal use of such pretrial discovery procedures as interrogatories, depositions, inspections, and demands for admissions. At the outset of our new system, fear was expressed that these pretrial procedures, especially discovery by deposition, would be abused. There have been occasional abuses, but they have been very few and in those instances ready relief has been afforded simply by the attorney's calling the situation to the attention of the trial judge. There can be no doubt that by these pretrial devices we have gone a long way in eliminating surprise. The trial judges now have it within their power to make sure that neither surprise nor technicalities win the battle. There are, of course, those who regret the passing of the "good old days" when one might turn a fast trick on one's adversary, but by and large there is an increas-

[17] Rule 1:27A provides: "The rules applicable to any court shall be considered as general rules for the government of the court and the conduct of causes; and as the design of them is to facilitate business and advance justice, they may be relaxed or dispensed with by the court in any instance where it shall be manifest to the court that a strict adherence to them will work surprise or injustice."

ing agreement on the fundamental thesis that a trial should be an orderly search for the true facts and the applicable law so that justice may be done in each case.

I have already mentioned the pretrial conference at some length. Its importance for improving the quality of trials, for shortening them, and for producing settlements by the voluntary agreement of the parties without pressure from the courts cannot be overestimated. Without it we could never have brought our calendars up to date in the time we did.

There are various other administrative rules, all of which have contributed in large measure to improving the work of the trial courts. For example, under the old practice motions were held in one court or another every day of the week with inevitable confusion and delay resulting; now they are all concentrated on Friday, the last regular court day of the week.[18] Again, cases that have been pending for more than six months without any proceedings having been taken are automatically listed by the clerk and are subject to dismissal for want of prosecution.[19]

Finally, we have eliminated another ancient source of untold delay—the sending of complicated matters to a referee for hearing without a jury. There is no more effective way of putting a case to sleep for an indefinite period of time than to send it to a busy lawyer as a referee. It is also as expensive as it is unnecessary. Even a

[18] Rule 1:28–3.
[19] Rule 1:30–3. Another rule, R.R. 1:30–4, makes a similar provision for the dismissal of inactive appeals to the County Courts.

drastic administrative rule [20] strictly limiting the matters in which a referee might be called did not put to rout this inveterate enemy of dispatch in the trial of cases. Only by requiring the approval of the chief justice for such references did they completely disappear, unmourned at least by trial lawyers who wish to get their cases disposed of. They know that there never has been a referee that proceeded at the pace required of proceedings before the trial judge.

In summary, in curing court congestion in New Jersey we have had a revolution in judicial and professional practice, a minor revolution which nevertheless has done much to increase public respect for law in our state. No longer is the successful litigant unnecessarily delayed. No longer do cases lie around law offices bringing in no income and serving no useful purpose. No longer does the trial judge needlessly carry a heavy pack of troubles on his back. The bench and the bar have won the respect of the public for industry and efficiency. Only the litigant who in bygone days profited by delay regrets the change, but we need not be concerned with his feelings. And what has been accomplished in New Jersey may be accomplished anywhere.

Despite allowance for all the time saved at a trial as a

[20] Rule 4:54–1 reads: "No reference for the hearing of a matter shall be made to a master, except under extraordinary circumstances, upon approval of the Chief Justice, or for the taking of a deposition, or as to matters heard by a standing master appointed by the Supreme Court. Any judge making a reference pursuant to this Rule shall submit to the Administrative Director of the Courts, together with his regular weekly report, a special report as to the status of the matter referred.

result of simplifying the pleadings and restating the issues, of obtaining admissions of facts and documents and of ordering trial briefs, it must still be admitted that we have much to learn from the English barristers and judges in expediting the conduct of a trial by the skillful examination of witnesses. It will probably be some time before our trial lawyers learn to confine their questions to relevant matters both on direct and cross-examination and limit their objections to meritorious matters, but with improved rules of evidence and a better teaching of trial technique in the law schools and continuous efforts on the part of the judge, the time required to try many cases can be substantially reduced. Moreover, instead of wasting time questioning every juror as to his fitness, often taking hours, days, or even weeks here to draw a jury, the clerk in the English courts in the relatively few civil cases where there is a jury simply calls twelve jurors to the box before the judge enters the courtroom. Some of our courts have progressed to the point where the judge questions the entire panel at once, asking all proper questions that counsel submit to him instead of wasting time in the individual questioning of jurors.

Using a jury in many law cases here is merely a habit. In England juries are sparingly used in civil matters. Many lawyers and litigants will waive a jury when they know the judge is capable, if the desirability of waiving a jury is called to their attention. Chief Justice Stern of Pennsylvania, when a judge of the Common Pleas Court in Philadelphia, cleared up a backlog of 3,000 cases largely by suggesting to counsel the possibility of waiving a jury in relatively unimportant negligence cases. The time saved in drawing a jury, in the opening and closing addresses to the jury, in eliminating argument on objections to evidence, and in shorter direct and cross-examination made it possible in a few hours to dispose of cases which otherwise would have taken days. Says Chief Justice Stern: "The plaintiffs expressed satisfaction because they were getting a prompt hearing of their cases with resulting prompt payments instead of being subjected to a long delay of years, and also because, in the overwhelming majority of the cases, no appeal from the verdict was or could be taken because of the absence of questions of law. On the other hand, the defendants were equally pleased because they felt protected from the danger of reckless and extravagant verdicts and were satisfied that the amounts found were fair and reasonable." [21]

Most of the devices I have mentioned making for the curing of congested calendars are of rather recent vintage in the law. Complete discovery at law in this country came only with the Federal Rules of Civil Procedure.[22] For centuries the law judges were merely allowed to adjudicate what came before them; they exercised no control over the progress of a case. It was not until the Judicature Acts [23] that the English law courts

[21] Letter to the writer.

[22] Part V, Depositions and Discovery, effective 1938.

[23] 7 Victoria, c. 66; 6 George V. c. 49 (Supreme Court of Judicature Act, 1925).

were given power to direct procedure to control the proper course of litigation, a power at first applied only to individual cases and only in recent years applied to an entire judicial system as a going concern.

I would not have you think that our interest in dispatch is confined to civil matters. It is equally important that the presiding judge in each county in New Jersey exercise as much control over the criminal calendar as he does over the civil list, that he keep a watchful eye on the operation of the municipal courts within his jurisdiction, and cause all appeals to be promptly disposed of. It is also essential that the county judges and juvenile court judges take an active interest in the work of the juvenile delinquency committees set up by rule of court [24] in each municipality and made up largely of laymen to aid the juvenile court judges at the local level. These committees are doing a work of inestimable value in solving a host of problems involving minor delinquency that would bring many children to court, thus freeing the judges to concentrate on the more serious cases in this field.

So far as I know, the courts are the only nationwide or statewide businesses that have ever attempted to function without any administrative machinery. The federal government in 1939 was the first to set up such an organization on a large scale in the establishment of the Administrative Office of the United States Courts.[25]

[24] Rule 6:2–2.
[25] Title 28, United States Code, Section 601 to 610.

New Jersey was the first state to do so by constitutional provision.[26] I will consider the New Jersey office first because the problems of a state administrative office are simpler than those of the federal office and more akin to what will probably be the development in other states. The movement is spreading; already California, Colorado, Connecticut, Iowa, Kentucky, Louisiana, Maryland, Michigan, Missouri, North Carolina, Oregon, Rhode Island, Virginia, the District of Columbia, and Puerto Rico have made provision for an administrative or similar office to assist in the various aspects of court administration.[27]

If a judicial system is to handle effectively its primary work of deciding cases and appeals, it must be provided with a sound administrative organization capable of establishing administrative policies and carrying them into effect. Such an organization is provided in New Jersey, and the record has demonstrated its utility. By the Constitution of 1947 the Supreme Court was granted the exclusive power not only to make rules of practice and procedure but also rules of administration for all of the courts in the state.[28] In matters of administration the Supreme Court therefore acts as the policy-making body for the judicial system, occupying a position in the administration of the courts comparable to that of the board of directors of a business corporation. The Constitution also provides that "the Chief Justice of the

[26] N.J. Const., 1947, Art. VI, Sec. VII, par. 1.
[27] See footnote 10 of Chapter I.
[28] N.J. Const., 1947, Art. VI, Sec. II, par. 3.

Supreme Court shall be the administrative head of all the courts" [29] and grants to him broad powers with respect to the assignment of judges.[30] His position, therefore, is comparable to that of chairman of the board and president of a business concern. He is concerned both with the establishment of policies and with their execution.

For the Supreme Court and the chief justice to exercise intelligently their policy-making powers and to enable the chief justice to carry adopted policies into effect, they must have an organization. This is primarily afforded by an Administrative Office of the Courts headed by a director who is appointed by and serves at the pleasure of the chief justice.[31] I shall shortly describe the operation and functions of this office in greater detail, but first I should mention other administrative measures that we have in addition found to be indispensable if desired policies are to be put into effect in every echelon of the courts. For each county a judge of the Superior Court has been designated as the assignment judge, and he is charged by rule of court with responsibility for the administration of both civil and criminal justice in every court in his county or counties.[32] He is the judicial officer on the scene who sees to it that the courts in his county or counties are functioning properly. Quarterly informal meetings of the assign-

[29] N.J. Const., 1947, Art. VI, sec. VII, par. 1.
[30] *ibid.*, Art. VI, sec. VII, par. 2; Art. XI, sec. 4, par. 5.
[31] *ibid.*, Art. VI, sec. VII, par. 1.
[32] Rule 1:29–1.

ment judges with the chief justice and the administrative director permit a two-way exchange of information and ideas. These meetings provide the medium for ironing out many practical problems that cannot be solved by rules, directives, reports, or correspondence.

In addition to the assignment judge, whose importance in the administration of the courts has constantly grown, in the local county district and municipal courts having more than one judge, one of them is designated as the presiding judge and is charged with the responsibility for the administration of his particular court.[33] In designating the assignment judges and the presiding judges the chief justice's primary concern is to select those judges who hold the greatest promise for dealing aggressively with administrative problems. This procedure, I believe, is far superior to that followed in the federal courts and in some other states where the senior judge in point of service is automatically charged with administrative responsibility, notwithstanding the fact that his interest and ability in matters of administration or even his physical capacity to handle the added work by reason of age and health may be clearly less than that of some younger judge in point of service.

By such an administrative organization, not only can desired improvements in the operation of the courts be swiftly and surely put into effect, but the time which an individual judge must devote to administrative matters rather than to his regular judicial duties is reduced to the minimum. Under this system the primary burden

[33] N.J.S. 2A:6–13 and 2A:8–19.

of handling the administrative detail incident to the running of the courts falls on the administrative director and his staff.

The enabling act creating the Administrative Office of the Courts in New Jersey gives the administrative director broad powers subject, of course, to the direction of the chief justice.[34] As now constituted, the office

[34] N.J.S. 2A:12–1 *et seq.* sec. 3, Functions of Director, provides:
"The director shall, subject to the direction of the chief justice, perform the following functions:

"(a) Examine the administrative methods, systems and activities of the judges, clerks, stenographic reporters and employees of the courts and their offices and make recommendations to the chief justice with respect thereto.

"(b) Examine the state of the dockets of the courts, secure information as to their needs for assistance, if any, prepare statistical data and reports of the business of the courts and advise the chief justice to the end that proper action may be taken.

"(c) Prepare and submit budget estimates of state appropriations necessary for the maintenance and operation of the courts and make recommendations with respect thereto.

"(d) File requests for appropriations or permission to spend, as request officer for the supreme and superior courts and, as approval officer, approve and sign all encumbrance requests and statements of indebtedness on behalf of said courts.

"(e) Make necessary arrangements for accommodations for the use of the supreme and superior courts and the clerks thereof and for the purchase, exchange, transfer and distribution of equipment and supplies for said courts and clerks.

"(f) Investigate and collect statistical data and make reports relating to the expenditures of public moneys, state, county and municipal, for the maintenance of the courts and the offices connected therewith.

"(g) Examine, from time to time, the operation of the courts, investigate complaints with respect thereto, and formulate and

consists of four lawyers, including the director, four secretaries, two clerks, and one bookkeeper. The administrative director and his assistants relieve the chief justice of the great mass of administrative detail that otherwise would prevent his doing his full share of the judicial work of the Supreme Court. I have fortunately had, successively, two very able lawyers as directors, both of whom were possessed of a natural instinct for sound business administration, and they in turn have been aided by an able and devoted staff.

The magnitude of the tasks performed by this small force will be better understood against the background of the extent of business done in our courts during the last year. The Supreme Court heard and decided 192 appeals, the Appellate Division of the Superior Court another 474 appeals, while the trial courts of general jurisdiction disposed of 12,973 law cases, 1,855 general equity cases, and 5,374 matrimonial cases, and the county district courts with limited civil jurisdiction 134,103 cases. On the criminal side 10,145 cases were disposed of in the trial courts with jurisdiction over indictable offenses, while during the year the municipal courts handled 894,946 cases, mostly involving traffic offenses.[35] Indeed, the collection of statistics for these

---

submit to the chief justice recommendations for the improvement thereof.

"(h) Act as secretary of the judicial conference held pursuant to supreme court rules.

"(i) Attend to such other matters as may be assigned by the chief justice."

[35] Annual Report of the Administrative Director, 1953–54.

courts is in itself a very considerable task. Sitting in the various courts are eighty full-time judges and more than five hundred part-time judges and magistrates throughout the state. There are also hundreds of clerks, sergeants-at-arms, secretaries, and court reporters looking to the Administrative Office for guidance. In describing the work of the Administrative Office we should bear in mind that while New Jersey is a small state ranking forty-fifth among the states in size, it ranks eighth in its population of 4,800,000 persons, being exceeded in density of population only by the District of Columbia and Rhode Island, and that while it is essentially an industrial state (the value of its manufactures is surpassed only by five other states) fifteen of its twenty-one counties are suburban or agricultural.

One of the functions of the Administrative Office is to assist the chief justice in the exercise of his authority to assign judges to the courts where they are most needed and to the kind of work they can do best. In order that this be done in an intelligent manner it is necessary to know the current status as well as the trends of judicial business in the entire state. To supply such up-to-the-minute data, reports are received weekly from the judges of all courts, except the judges of municipal courts who report monthly. These reports show the number of hours the judges spent on the bench, the number of trials, pretrials, and motions heard, and the number of cases and motions heard in which decision was reserved. A weekly summary of this data is prepared for the chief justice. From the clerks of all the trial courts come monthly reports on the civil calendars. Similar reports are made by the county prosecutors and county clerks on criminal cases. Summaries of these reports are prepared and furnished the chief justice and associate justices of the Supreme Court three or four days after the end of each month. These reports and summaries enable the chief justice to transfer judges from one division of a court to another or from one county to another to prevent the piling up of cases in any county and to keep all judges fully employed. In making assignments he chooses those judges who can best be spared from their own county or division.

In addition to the reports mentioned above, statistics are collected on many other facets of the operation of the courts and are published by the administrative director in monthly, quarterly, and annual reports to the Supreme Court. As the need appears, special reports are requested by the Administrative Office and special studies are conducted on particular problems. With such information available, the chief justice and the Supreme Court can take appropriate steps to meet new situations before they become troublesome, and the entire judicial system can be administered in an intelligent, business-like fashion.

Primary among the functions of the Administrative Office is the handling of fiscal and business affairs. The director is charged with the preparation of the budget for the courts, a matter of close to $3,000,000 annually. This necessitates participation in budget hearings before the director of budget and accounting and, when required, before the joint appropriations committee of the legislature. Furthermore, as request-and-approval officer for the judicial department, the administrative director has control over all expenditures of appropriated funds and is reponsible for the maintenance of adequate books and records with respect thereto. It is also his responsibility to make the necessary arrangements for courtrooms, chambers, and offices for the use of the courts and their judges and clerks and to secure for them all necessary equipment and supplies. The director also supervises the investment and management of funds paid into court of which the chief justice is, by law, the trustee.

Another function of the administrative director is the publication of court opinions. The director is a member of a committee appointed by the Supreme Court to pass upon the opinions of all judges, except the justices of the Supreme Court, to determine whether they should be published. The negotiation of the contract with the printer and the arrangements for the editing of opinions are worked out under the supervision of the administrative director. Recently a program of distribution of opinions prior to publication has been instituted and the judges now receive within a few days of the date they are filed copies of all opinions that are approved for publication.

The administrative director also serves as the public relations officer of the courts. General public respect for law depends in a large measure upon the efficiency with which the courts administer the law. The Administrative Office, with full possession of the facts, is the natural agency for the distribution of press releases on the work of the judiciary. On occasion the administrative director can with propriety meet unwarranted criticism leveled at the courts, something a judge is not in a position to do.

Not the least in importance of the obligations of the administrative director and his staff are the supplying of information and the investigation of complaints. Inquiries pertaining to the courts are routed to his office and there receive the same careful attention whether they come from judges, law enforcement officers, lawyers, or laymen. It is a matter of considerable pride and satisfaction that many inquiries have come from high officials in the courts and governments of other states and foreign jurisdictions. Similarly, complaints addressed to the courts are given prompt attention. While experience has demonstrated that most complaints are baseless and the work of disappointed litigants or cranks, each is investigated and the complainant advised of the result. When a complaint is found to be justified, every effort is made to correct the situation. The fact that there is an agency to which complaints may be directed and which will take such steps as are warranted has contributed much to the confidence that the public places in our courts.

Last, but among the more important duties of the administrative director, is acting as secretary to the Judicial Conference and the Municipal Magistrates Conference, which I have mentioned before. The Administrative Office also assists the various committees of these conferences in their work and handles all the arrangements in connection with the staging of the conferences themselves. In addition, each year a number of other conferences, such as those of the Chancery Division judges, the matrimonial judges, the presiding judges of the county district courts and, as mentioned before, the assignment judges, are arranged at which selected groups of judges discuss with the chief justice in detail their peculiar problems and at which the policies of the Supreme Court on various administrative matters can be fully explained.

In the light of my experience I find it difficult to understand how any statewide judicial establishment can function efficiently without a judge, preferably the chief justice, as the administrative head of the courts, without senior judges, assignment judges, and presiding judges charged with responsibility for the supervision of the work of their respective courts, and without an administrative office such as I have been describing.

When we turn to the administration of the United States courts we are dealing with big business indeed. In 1954 the federal courts were manned by 366 judges and over 4,100 other court officers and employees.[36] The Congress for the fiscal year 1954 appropriated in excess of $26,000,000 for their operation.[37] Their activities extend through the forty-eight states, the District of Columbia, and all the territories and insular possessions.

[36] *Annual Report of the Director of the Administrative Office of the United States Courts for 1954*, p. 58.

[37] Total appropriations for the courts of appeal, district courts, and other judicial services (not including the Supreme Court, the Court of Customs and Patent Appeals, the Customs Court, the Court of Claims, the Tax Court, and the Court of Military Ap-

Yet only during the past twenty-five years has any attempt at all been made to apply to their operation even the most basic principles of sound business administration. As Chief Judge John J. Parker of the Court of Appeals for the Fourth Circuit, has so forcefully stated: "Until a few years ago, the federal courts had the worst organization and procedure to be found in the country, if not in the world. The conformity act designed to conform the practice of the federal courts to that of the states in which they were sitting had failed of its purpose; and what was being administered was an antiquated, hybrid system, full of pitfalls and technicalities. There was no adequate organization of judicial manpower and no supervision whatever of judicial administration." [38]

The Judiciary Act of 1789 [39] first established the federal court structure, but thereafter it was left to grow like Topsy without effective thought toward developing it into an integrated, efficiently operated system. In 1850 a law [40] was passed providing that when the judge of a district was unable to sit by reason of

peals) amounted to $26,041,870 for the fiscal year 1954 and $28,214,525 has been requested for the fiscal year 1955. *Hearings before the Subcommittee on Legislative-Judiciary Appropriations of the Committee on Appropriations, House of Representatives, 83rd Congress, 2nd Session,* p. 1 (1954).

[38] In an address on "The Federal Judiciary" delivered at the Centennial Commemoration Exercises of the College of Law of the Tulane University of Louisiana on April 29, 1948, printed in 22 *Tulane Law Review* 569, at 574 (June, 1948).

[39] 1 Stat. 73.

[40] 9 Stat. 442.

sickness or disability, the judge of another district within the same circuit might be assigned to act in his stead, and in 1907 the Chief Justice was authorized to assign a judge from one circuit to another if no judge was available there.[41] But these powers were seldom utilized and were obviously of no value in welding together the numerous federal courts scattered across a growing country.

The first important step in the integration of the federal courts did not come until 1922 when Congress, in an effort to tighten enforcement of the Volstead Act, passed the Daugherty bill [42] authorizing the assignment of a judge to another circuit when the resident judge was "unable to perform speedily the work of his district" by reason of "the accumulation or urgency of business." Of far more importance, however, was the provision establishing the Judicial Conference of Senior Circuit Judges grafted on the measure largely at the insistence of Chief Justice Taft. In speaking before the Judicial Section of the American Bar Association in 1921 when the Daugherty bill was still pending, he called attention to the promise it held for the courts:

"It provides for annual meetings of the Chief Justice and the senior circuit judges from the nine circuits, and the Attorney General, to consider required reports from district judges and clerks as to the business in their respective districts, with a view to mak-

[41] 34 Stat. 1417.
[42] 42 Stat. 838.

ing a yearly plan for the massing of the new and old judicial forces of the United States in these districts all over the country where the arrears are threatening to interfere with the usefulness of the courts. It is the introduction into our courts of an executive principle to secure effective teamwork. Heretofore each judge has paddled his own canoe and has done the best he could with his district. He has been subject to little supervision, if any. Judges are men, and are not so keenly charged with the duty of constant labor that the stimulus of an annual inquiry into what they are doing may not be helpful. With such mild visitation he is likely to cooperate much more readily in an organized effort to get rid of business and do justice than under the go-as-you-please system of our present Federal judges, which has left unemployed in easy districts a good deal of the judicial energy that may now be usefully applied elsewhere." [43]

In addition to considering the redistribution of judicial personnel to relieve congestion, which at the time was envisioned as its primary purpose and has since proved to be the area of its least effectiveness, the Judicial Conference was empowered to "submit such suggestions to the various courts as may seem in the interest of uniformity and expedition of business." This latter power has proved progressively more important and by its exercise the Judicial Conference has made substantial contributions to improving the work of the federal

[43] 5 *Journal Am. Jud. Soc.* 37 (Aug. 1921).

courts. The discussions of the presiding judges of the eleven circuits at these annual meetings have resulted in a variety of recommendations for the improvement of the federal courts in the fields of procedure, administration, and legislation, not the least of them being the support it gave to the Civil Rules Act [44] vesting in the Supreme Court the power to prescribe by rule procedure in the courts. Thereafter the Judicial Conference assisted the Supreme Court in the formulation of the Federal Rules of Civil Procedure, as well as the Federal Rules of Criminal Procedure.[45]

It was too much to expect, however, that twelve judges meeting annually in Washington and engaged the rest of the year in performing their regular judicial duties could by themselves superintend and administer the vast system of federal courts. Obviously they could deal effectively only with matters of general policy, and even then they lacked both necessary information about the operation of the courts and administrative facilities essential to effectuate decisions.

It now seems almost unbelievable that until the Administrative Office Act of 1939 [46] the Federal courts had no business department of their own, but were dependent entirely on the attorney general and the Department of Justice, representing the chief litigant in these courts, for the conduct of all of their business affairs, from the purchasing of pencils to the presentation of the judicial

[44] 48 Stat. 1064 (1934).
[45] 54 Stat. 688 (1940).
[46] 53 Stat. 1223–1225.

budget to the appropriate committees of Congress. Credit for ending this obviously improper relationship and for bringing about the establishment of the Administrative Office of the United States Courts belongs chiefly to one man, Attorney General Homer Cummings, whose views were succinctly stated in a communication to Congress:

> "I am convinced that the functions of the judiciary cannot be performed efficiently and expeditiously unless the courts are equipped with proper and adequate administrative machinery which they themselves can control and for which they will be responsible. The independence of the judiciary would seem to require that its administrative work should not be handled by one of the executive departments, or be under the control of the chief litigant in the Federal courts." [47]

Never before in the history of the Federal government had any department voluntarily relinquished so much power. Indeed, at one time the acceptance of these responsibilities had to be urged on the Supreme Court. This act was quite aptly described by Judge Parker as "the most important piece of legislation affecting the judiciary since the Judiciary Act of 1789." [48]

The Administrative Office Act did more than establish an agency within the judicial department to manage the business affairs of the courts and to collect information

[47] Swisher, *Selected Papers of Homer Cummings*, 225, (1939).
[48] Parker, "The Federal Judiciary," 22 *Tulane L. Rev.* 569 at 575 (June, 1948).

and statistical data with respect to the courts. It expanded the powers and responsibilities of the Judical Conference of Senior Circuit Judges and extended the administrative organization to the local level by providing for judicial councils and judicial conferences in each circuit. "While the new system was intended to be of aid in these matters of apparatus [the handling of the business affairs of the court]," as Chief Justice Hughes pointed out, "the chief objective was to promote promptness and efficiency in the disposition of litigation." [49] Unhappily this objective has not been accomplished, for reasons which will be discussed subsequently.

Quite obviously the Judicial Conference, meeting as it does only for a few days two or three times a year, cannot discharge its duties without assistance. For this reason under the leadership of Chief Justice Hughes it developed to the fullest extent the committee system and has continued to make the maximum use of this method of diversifying its work. Judges of the various courts of appeals and district courts are called on extensively to serve on the various committees, and in this fashion not only is the work load widely distributed but, more significantly, the Judicial Conference utilizes to the fullest extent the many special talents of the federal judges and gains the advantage of the perspective which broad representation always affords. Regrettably the committee reports are not included in the published reports of the meetings of the Judicial Conference, and as a result

[49] Address before the American Law Institute, meeting at Washington, D.C., May 6, 1941.

all of them are not readily available for study by those who are interested in judicial administration. It would indeed be helpful if the Administrative Office of the United States or some other appropriate organization were to collect and publish these reports so that the valuable information contained in them is not lost.

While the Administrative Office Act greatly increased the duties of the Judicial Conference of Senior Circuit Judges, that body has not been vested with the executive power necessary to accomplish the Act's primary purpose, the elimination of congestion in the courts. Largely as the result of the view expressed by Chief Justice Hughes that the Chief Justice and the senior circuit judges should not be unduly oppressed by administrative duties, the Judicial Conference in September 1938 recommended that the primary supervisory powers over the district court judges in the several circuits be vested in judicial councils,[50] made up of the circuit judges, and appropriate provision in the then pending legislation [51] was made to adopt this recommendation.

Some of the circuit councils have served a definite purpose by studying a wide variety of problems encountered in the day to day operation of the courts. For instance, the minutes of the meetings of the Judicial Council for the Third Circuit indicate that it has considered some thirty-five different subjects relating to the

[50] Report of the Judicial Conference, September Session 1938, printed in the Annual Report of the Attorney General for the Fiscal Year 1938, p. 24.

[51] S. 3212 (75th Cong.), reintroduced in amended form as S.188 (76th Cong.).

burden of judicial business, court personnel, procedure, and miscellaneous other matters.[52] They have likewise proved valuable by giving to the Judicial Conference of the United States, as it is now called, a better understanding of the points of view and problems of the different sections of the country. But in the fundamental objective of eliminating congestion and delay and of equalizing the work of the district court judges they have been a dismal failure.

The Report for 1954 of the Director of the Administrative Office of the United States Courts calls attention to the congestion in many districts with the resultant hardship to litigants, especially those of modest means, and reveals that the median length of time to get a case disposed of by trial varies all the way from 4.8 months in the Northern District of Texas to 45.0 months in the Southern District of New York, and that as a rule it takes several times longer to get a case tried in one district as compared to another even within the same circuit.[53] That the total volume of judicial business and the average case load per judge is continually increasing is of no moment here, for certainly the citizens of one district are just as much entitled to their day in court as the citizens of any other district. Whatever the reasons—I will suggest a few later—the judicial councils in the cir-

[52] Memorandum on the Powers of the Judicial Councils, prepared by W. H. Speck of the Administrative Office of the United States Courts, July 13, 1949, Appendix A.

[53] Annual Report of the Director of the Administrative Office of the United States.

cuits have not lived up to expectations in eliminating delay.

For many years prior to 1939 in some of the circuits, notably the Fourth Circuit presided over by Chief Judge Parker, annual conferences of judges and lawyers provided a convenient forum for the discussion of the problems of the courts. The success of these conferences was so great that a provision was included in the Administrative Office Act requiring in every circuit an annual conference of all the circuit and district judges and others designated by the Court of Appeals in each circuit "for the purpose of considering the business of the courts and advising means of improving the administration of justice within such circuit." [54] Unlike the Judicial Conference of the United States, the circuit conferences have no authority, but some of them have proved useful vehicles for the exchange of ideas, grievances, and suggestions, particularly in those circuits where representatives of the bar have been encouraged to participate.

The keystone of the Act of August 7, 1939, as its title indicates, was the establishment of the Administrative Office of the United States Courts. Now concluding its fifteenth year, it has amply demonstrated its usefulness by the efficient and expeditious handling of the business affairs of the federal courts and by making available periodically a storehouse of information with respect to their operation. In addition, it has been of tremendous assistance to the committees of the Judicial Conference both by reason of the special studies it has made and the

[54] 28 U.S.C. §333.

service rendered individually by its staff. The success of the Administrative Office has also been of incidental although not inconsiderable value in providing the states with a concrete example of the benefits to be gained by placing the judiciary on a businesslike basis. In light of the federal experience, it is inconceivable why so few states have as yet seen fit to follow suit.

It is not necessary here to detail the origin, organization, and operation of the Administrative Office or to recount the specific contributions it has made to the improvement of the federal judiciary. That task has been fully and expertly performed by its director, Henry P. Chandler, and others of his efficient staff in a number of speeches and articles, many of which have been published in widely read legal periodicals.[55]

With a Judicial Conference of the United States, with judicial councils and judicial conferences in the several circuits, and with an efficient Administrative Office, all created for the primary purpose of eliminating the delays in the federal courts, it is natural to inquire why so little progress has been made. The obvious answer generally given is that the Congress has failed to provide a

[55] Chandler, "Making the Judicial Machinery Function Efficiently," 22 *N.Y.U.Q. Rev.* 445 (July, 1947); Chandler, "The Administration of the Federal Courts," 13 *Law and Contemporary Problems* 182 (Winter, 1948); Shafroth, "Federal Judicial Statistics," 13 *Law and Contemporary Problems* 200 (Winter, 1948); Tolman, "The Administration of the Federal Courts," 37 *A.B.A.J.* 31 (Jan., 1951); Tolman, "The Administration of the Federal Courts: A Review of Progress During 1950–1951," 38 *A.B.A.J.* 127 (Feb., 1952); Speck, "Statistics for the United States Courts: An Indispensable Tool for Judicial Management," 38 *A.B.A.J.* 936 (Nov., 1952).

sufficient number of judges in the districts where congestion exists, but this is at best only a partial answer. To an outsider who is not unfamiliar with the problems of judicial administration, three other reasons suggest themselves.

First, the federal judicial system lacks an effective executive head. Under the present administrative organization executive authority and responsibility are primarily vested in the circuit judicial councils, each composed of a number of judges. Such a situation is inherently unsound, for while a group of individuals lends itself well to the establishment of policies, it is not adapted to the task of seeing that they are carried out. There is no more reason for believing that a judicial system can operate properly without an executive head than there is for believing that the executive department of a government could function effectively with a cabinet but no president or governor, or that a large business concern could withstand competition with a board of directors but no president. It is eminently desirable that to the fullest extent possible the administration of the federal courts be decentralized, and although the Judicial Conference of the United States and the circuit councils and conferences most certainly have their place, they are no substitute for an effective executive. However much the Chief Justice and the chief judges in the circuits may personally wish to avoid the onerous duty, they should individually be made the responsible executives operating under policies laid down by the Judicial Conference and the judicial councils in the circuits.

Second, the broad authority already vested in the

Chief Justice and the chief judges in the circuits has not been fully utilized. The Report of the Director of the Administrative Office of the United States Courts for 1954 [56] indicates that during the year only seven circuit judges were assigned to other circuits and only thirteen district court judges assigned to other circuits. The report contains no information on assignments from one district to another within a circuit, but I am told that they are not numerous. Why then has there been such a reluctance to exercise these assignment powers? The reasons are probably several.

The Chief Justice and the chief judges have not been generally considered individually responsible for the exercise of these powers nor for the untoward conditions that continue to exist. The establishment in fact of the Chief Justice and the chief judges as responsible executive heads, as previously indicated, would eliminate these restraining factors.

The practice has grown up in the federal courts that judges are assigned outside their districts only if they consent. Judge Alexander Holtzoff, then appearing as a representative of the Department of Justice, made this plain at the Senate subcommittee hearings on the Administrative Office bill fifteen years ago: "If a district judge indicates a reluctance to take an assignment outside of his own district, there is nothing the senior circuit judge can do about it. I understand that the custom has been for the senior circuit judge to obtain the con-

[56] Annual Report of the Director of the Administrative Office of the United States Courts for 1954, pp. 9–10.

sent of the district judge when he proposes to send him to another district. Legally, he does not have to do it, but I imagine it is the safe thing to do." [57]

I am informed that this custom has continued to this day. From the standpoint of the individual judge this deference to his desires is indeed admirable, but has not the time long since arrived when the personal convenience of the judges must be subordinated to the critical needs of the litigants whom the courts are intended to serve? A business concern does not hesitate to shift its executive personnel to the areas where they are most needed, and there is no good reason why judges should be immune to similar treatment. The remedy here will not come easily, however, and before it can even be hoped for, provision must be made for fully reimbursing the judges for all expenses reasonably incurred in connection with their assignment. It is enough to subject a judge to inconvenience; it is too much to burden him in addition with a pecuniary loss. In his reports the director of the Administrative Office has repeatedly called attention to this situation, but without success.

The statistical data collected and published by the Administrative Office of the Courts provides valuable information on virtually every facet of the courts' business, but there is one significant gap. No information is collected on the amount of time each judge devotes to his judicial duties. We may know how many cases, by type,

[57] Hearings before Subcommittee of the Committee on the Judiciary, U.S. Senate, 76th Cong., 1st Sess. on S. 188, April 4 and 5, 1939, pp. 35–36.

a judge has disposed of and how many cases of various kinds he has remaining on his calendar, but if we do not also know the amount of time the judge is actually putting in we cannot intelligently determine whether he is really in need of assistance or available for assignment elsewhere. If the maximum use is to be made of all available judicial manpower, it is essential that every judge be required to render a weekly report of his activities for the benefit of the judge holding the power of assignment. This reform will come hard, but once instituted the evils conjured up by those who opposed it will prove to be purely imaginary. Among its many merits, it protects a hard-working judge from being imposed on by others who might otherwise be less devoted to duty.

Third, there has been a decided reluctance in the federal courts to make mandatory those practices and procedures which have been conclusively demonstrated to be of value. Probably the prime example of this is the pretrial conference. In 1944 the Judicial Conference approved the conclusions of its Committee to Study the Use of Pretrial Procedure in the Federal Courts to the effect that "every civil case in which issue has been joined should be pretried before it is assigned for trial, unless there are special circumstances which render such a conference unnecessary or inexpedient, or unless the case is one of such a nature that it appears that pretrial would be of no advantage." [58] Four years later the committee pointed out that in only about 25% of the federal

[58] Report of the Judicial Conference, September Session, 1944, p. 20.

district courts were pretrial conferences an accepted part of the regular procedure and accordingly it re-affirmed its previous recommendation.[59] In the report of the Judicial Conference that year it was stated that the committee "emphasized the fact that ten years of experience in the federal courts has demonstrated be-yond peradventure that pretrial procedures result not only in greater efficiency in the judicial processes, but in great economies in time and money for the courts, the litigants, and the public." [60] Yet still another four years later, in 1952, the committee reported that pretrial con-ferences were being used regularly in most civil cases in only between one-third and one-half of the districts.[61] Is there any good reason why pretrial conferences should not long ago have been made mandatory and this continued disregard of the best interests of the litigant and the public put to an end by a simple rule of court?

In marked contrast to the administrative establish-ments of the United States and New Jersey courts is the act for "court administration" recently enacted in New York on the recommendation of the Temporary Commission on the Courts.[62] I find it difficult to en-vision a legislative scheme less likely to achieve admin-istrative efficiency in the courts; it inescapably calls

[59] Report of the Committee on Pretrial Procedure, Sept. 15, 1948, pp. 2, 6.

[60] Report of the Judicial Conference of the United States, Sep-tember 27–29, 1948, p. 36.

[61] Report of the Judicial Conference of the United States, Sep-tember 22–24, 1952, p. 20.

[62] 1955, ch. 869.

to mind the statement of a well known member of the House of Commons in quite a different connection: "Nothing is as dangerous in a democracy as a safeguard which appears to be adequate but is really a façade." [63]

The act creates a judicial conference of nine, consisting of the chief judge of the court of appeals as chairman, the presiding justice of the appellate division of each of the four departments of the supreme court and one of the justices of the supreme court in each of the four departments [64] to be chosen for a two year tenure by the supreme court justices who are trial judges.[65] If the act were aimed at action, which, as I will show, it is not, the mere presence in the conference of four trial judges chosen as these four are, would serve to maintain the *status quo* indefinitely. The difficulties of judicial administration are chiefly at the trial level, and judges rarely vote to reform themselves. But to make assurance of inaction doubly sure, it is provided that the chairman and the ranking minority member of the committees on the judiciary and on codes of each branch of the legislature, eight in all, are to be given notice of each meeting and they may attend and make recommendations.[66] The legislature was obviously unwilling to trust a body of judges to perform even the limited functions assigned to it without legislative chaperons.

[63] Miss Ellen Wilkerson, M.P. in *Committee on Members' Powers Report* (1936, Cmd. 4060), 138.

[64] sec. 230.

[65] sec. 231.

[66] sec. 232.

Inasmuch as the matters committed to the conference relate solely to the courts, it would seem that respect for the doctrine of the separation of powers should have dictated that the legislative branch should not intrude itself in matters primarily of judicial concern.

The act then provides that the conference shall meet semi-annually and at such other times as the chairman shall designate,[67] as if it would be possible really to attend to the involved problems of judicial administration existing in New York state in any such occasional way. Judicial administration, like the administration of any other statewide business, is a full-time day-by-day and often hour-by-hour job. But a study of the powers of the conference reveals that, although the act mentions the words "administration," "administrative," and "administrator" frequently, it is not at all an administrative body, but essentially a *study group*. Substantially all its powers are "to study and to make recommendations," and there its power stops. To appreciate this one must examine its powers carefully. It is authorized:

> *"To study and to make recommendations* with respect to the organization, jurisdiction, procedures and rules, and the administrative . . . practices of all the courts . . . ;"[68]

> "To collect, compile and publish statistics . . . ;"[69]

[67] sec. 232.
[68] sec. 233 (1).
[69] sec. 233 (2).

"To make *such studies and recommendations as it may deem advisable* with respect to fiscal matters, pending legislation and court decisions affecting the administration of justice; [70]

"To receive, and, *to the extent it may deem advisable,* to investigate and *make recommendations* with respect to criticisms and suggestions from any source pertaining to the administration of justice; [71]

"*To study and to make recommendations* regarding the relief of congestion in particular courts; [72]

"To establish methods for the preservation, maintenance and disposition of court records; [73]

". . . to submit to the legislature and to the governor an annual report of the proceedings of the conference and of the business transacted by the courts during the preceding year together with any *recommendations* for legislation; [74]

"*To study and make recommendations* as to the transfer to the conference, in the interests of uniformity and efficiency, of administrative functions now performed by the judicial and non-judicial personnel of any court." [75]

[70] sec. 233 (3).
[71] sec. 233 (4).
[72] sec. 233 (5).
[73] sec. 233 (7).
[74] sec. 233 (8).
[75] sec. 233 (10).

These are not the kinds of powers regularly granted to the board of directors of a corporation doing a great statewide business in the interest of its stockholders. On the contrary, these provisions embody one of the oldest of delaying tactics known to legislative practice, the appointment of a committee to study and report next year; only here the conference will go on studying and recommending without limit in time, but with carefully circumscribed limitations as to the subject matter of its study and recommendations.

Two grants of power deserve especial comment. At one point it almost seems as if the conference were being given something approaching genuine administrative powers when it is empowered:

> "To recommend the assignment of judges and justices for service in the same court or other courts as the state of judicial business warrants . . ." [76]

but then in the same section even this hope is taken away:

> ". . . no justice of the supreme court shall be assigned outside the judicial department in which he was elected or appointed without the approval of the presiding justice of the appellate division of such department."

Thus we find frozen into legislation the vicious judicial protocol that we have seen by custom prevents the effective transfer of judges in the federal government.

[76] sec. 233 (6).

This provision would serve effectively to block the transfer of judges from adjoining counties as, for example, from Westchester County to the Bronx.

The other provision deals with the rule-making power. New York, it is everywhere conceded, has one of the most complicated codes of procedure to be found in this country. Its manifold shortcomings have been inveighed against so long and so often that it is quite unnecessary to cite authority for its deficiencies. Here at least one might have expected an outright delegation of rule-making power to the judicial conference, but one may read the grant of power to the conference in this respect without ever suspecting that at present procedure is the creature of the legislature!

> "At such times as it may deem advisable, to recommend, in the interests of uniformity and efficiency, to any court *or to any body* vested with the rule-making power for any court any changes in rules, practices or methods of administering judicial business." [77]

The legislature is not even mentioned; here we have a legislative façade, if ever there was one. I know it may be contended that this paragraph is intended to pave the way for recommendations for future changes in the exercise of the rule-making power "at such times as it may deem advisable," to quote the act, but what chance is there of attaining even a free discussion of the matter in the conference in the presence of the eight legislative policemen from the judiciary and codes committees?

But it will be said there surely must be some admin-

[77] sec. 233 (9).

istrative powers granted to the judicial conference for it is solemnly provided that

> "The chairman of the conference shall exercise and perform such administrative functions as may be prescribed by the conference during such periods as the conference is not in session." [78]

and provision is made for a state administrator for the conference and a deputy administrator in each of the four departments, the state administrator to be appointed on the nomination of the chairman, the four deputies on the nomination of the presiding justices of the appellate divisions of each judicial department with the approval of his colleagues.[79] But the state administrator and the four deputy administrators, who incidentally have no relation or responsibility to him but function solely with the departmental committees I shall describe, have no administrative duties whatsoever. The legislature has merely purloined a term that has a definite, known meaning in the nineteen states [80] that have administrative establishments and misappropriated it for an office that is utterly without administrative powers. Despite the use of language of administration with respect to the chairman and the state and deputy administrators, nowhere in the act are any of them or the conference itself accorded administrative powers except in one minor particular to be mentioned presently.

[78] sec. 234.
[79] sec. 233 (11).
[80] sec. 235.

The act then provides for "departmental committees for court administration" (again the language of administration without the reality) in each of the four judicial departments, "which shall consist of the presiding justice as chairman, the other member of the conference from within the department, a justice of the supreme court, not a member of the conference and not designated to an appellate division or the court of appeals, from each judicial district within the department chosen by the justices of the supreme court of each of said districts, . . . such judges or justices of other courts in that department as may be designated by the conference" and a varying number of members of the bar from each judicial district.[81] Each departmental committee

". . . shall examine the facilities, operation and budgets of the courts in its department, and shall formulate procedures and make recommendations to the conference and appropriate authorities for the improvement of the administration of justice therein. Each departmental committee shall submit annually to the conference a report on the effectiveness of the procedures and practices of the courts within its department and its recommendations and those of the departmental conference within the department with respect to general improvements in the conduct of the business of the courts therein." [82]

[81] sec. 235.
[82] sec. 237.

Here, again, we find no administrative powers, but merely the power to study and to make recommendations as in the case of the judicial conference itself.

Finally each departmental committee is given authority

". . . to call an annual conference within its department for the purpose of considering the business of the courts therein and proposing means for their improvement, and may invite thereto representatives of the bench, bar and legislature and others concerned with the administration of justice." [83]

These departmental committees and departmental conferences would be highly useful if they were reporting to a body which had real authority either to legislate or administer, but obviously they cannot, except under the rarest circumstances, accomplish much merely as recommenders to recommenders. Meantime the courts of New York continue without any supervision at the state level or any effective administration at the departmental level, though anyone reading the act in cursory fashion without either knowing the local situation or the capacity of judges for maintaining the *status quo* or of lawyers for yielding to them, might well imagine that a great reform had been set in motion by the act. It was the example of New York a century ago that thrust on most of the states of the country an elective judiciary (a dubious distinction which, as we have seen, these states share only with

[83] sec. 238.

Soviet Russia and its satellites). It was New York a century ago that set the example that has been followed in so many states of a constantly enlarging and continually amended legislative code of procedure, which has long hampered the judiciary in eliminating technicalities and surprise and in deciding controversies on the merits. The influence of New York may still be potent with the legal profession and the legislatures in other states. If any of them is tempted to follow this latest example of New York in the field of "judicial reform," it should at least do so with its eyes open and aware from the outset of the ineffectiveness of the reform proposed.

Nor can it be said that the New York legislature did not understand the problem before it, for it had at its disposal, among other sources of information, the volume of the Association of the Bar of the City of New York entitled *Bad Housekeeping; The Administration in the New York Courts*. In Chapter VII it set forth a plan for the administration of the New York courts. In contrast to the "study group" created by the New York legislature, the Association would permit the conference "to make all necessary orders within constitutional and statutory limitations, for expediting the business of the courts, and to require all judicial and non-judicial personnel of the courts to carry out those orders"; would require the director "to supervise the offices of the clerks, and other clerical and administrative personnel of the courts; prescribe fiscal and accounting procedures," and "to fix the compensation of all employees of the courts," and "to determine the qualifications requisite for all employees of the courts"; and would require the departmental administrative committees "to assure that the programs and policies promulgated by the judicial conference and the administrative office are carried into effect; and to that end the judiciary within each department would be required to comply with the directives of the committee." The new bill has no provision even remotely resembling such powers. The nearest it comes to giving the judicial conference power is with respect to the relatively unimportant matter of the preservation and disposition of court records where they are allowed "to establish methods." The various objections raised in *Bad Housekeeping* to the present court administration in New York can continue under the new act with even the most competent staff, because they have no authority to do anything to correct the situation except, of course, to study and recommend. The lack of coordination of judicial assignments, discussed in Chapter II of *Bad Housekeeping,* can continue; the disparities in policies of staffing and paying judges and court personnel described in Chapters III and IV of the Association's book will not be changed by any power given to the administrative machinery under the act. The system by which the New York courts are now financed is not altered. Thus it seems clear that the new law of itself promises nothing new or different because it does not supply what is clearly the greatest need and certainly the need it was supposed to fill—a system of court administration.

If improvement in judicial administration comes in New York it will not be because of this law, but rather because of the efforts made by the presiding justices without legislation. This is especially true of the First Department where Presiding Justice David W. Peck has achieved remarkable results in relieving the congestion of court calendars largely through his personal influence, but nothing comparable to what he could do if he or the chief judge were clothed with adequate authority. Meanwhile, as we have seen, litigation in New York continues years in arrears [84] as it has for a hundred years or more [85] despite a score or more of commission and committee reports.[86] It is becoming increasingly apparent that if judicial reform is to come in New York it must come as in England and in New Jersey through a popular movement of laymen led or advised by a few courageous and informed judges and lawyers.

Fortunately in the other states which have set up administrative offices, progress is being made in varying degrees. Ultimately the degree of success attained in any jurisdiction depends on the attitude of the bench, the bar and the public toward the courts.

I believe that the undue delays of the law can be eliminated, if we are willing to keep continuously in mind that the courts exist for the benefit of the state and of the litigants, not the judges and the lawyers. If we are not willing to act on this obvious principle, the

[84] See footnote 1 of Chapter IV.
[85] See footnote 2 of Chapter IV.
[86] See footnote 3 of Chapter IV.

art of judicial administration will continue in a prolonged and puny infancy despite the best possible administrative offices. With its full recognition, however, all of the shortcomings of judicial personnel, of procedure, and of administration can readily be overcome. Our first task, then, is to obtain general acquiescence in this sound principle, and here the law schools of the country can make a great contribution. Instead of teaching procedure, as so many of them do, as a set of technical rules quite unrelated to what actually goes on in the courtroom, do they not owe a duty to tell their students from the outset about the basic problems we have been considering, so that they will not become part of the professional forces of indifference and inertia that have so often prevented the law from performing its proper function in society? In so doing, the law schools will be speeding the day when we may turn our attention to the modernization and simplification of the substantive law to meet the needs of the times.

CHAPTER V

Modernizing the Law
through Law Centers

I HAVE already dwelt on the pressing need to improve judicial personnel (not merely judges, but jurors as well), to simplify the structure of the judicial system and the procedure followed in the courts so that the decisions of cases on technicalities or by surprise may be avoided and so that procedure may become a means of achieving justice rather than an end in itself; and finally, to eliminate the age-old vice of undue delays in the law through effective management of the judicial system. I have maintained—and I trust I have demonstrated—that all these highly desirable objectives in the administration of justice are readily attainable, once the legal profession in all its branches realizes their necessity, or failing such support, once the public wants them enough to work for them in the face of the opposition of the legal profession. In some states a long time may pass before it is clear that the bench, the bar, and the law schools are not willing to assume their responsibility for these reforms. It may take a long time for the public in such states to realize that the legal profession has ignored its natural responsibility and intends to continue permanently in default, thus confessing professional bankruptcy, and that therefore the public must act. But in either event, once *that* question is resolved, the amount of time and effort required for either the profession or the public to achieve the desired goal is relatively small in comparison with reforms in many other fields. The greatest difficulty has always been to decide who is to do the job, the legal profession or the public.

The reforms we have been considering all lie in the broad field of what is often termed the machinery of the administration of justice, a field in which the shortcomings of the law are peculiarly irritating to litigants and the public generally. In marked contrast to these is the problem of the vast body of substantive law, the problem of the content of laws as distinguished from the means of enforcing them. The public correctly believes that the machinery of the administration of justice can and should be simplified and improved. On the other hand, popular complaints concerning the substantive law are far less common than those concerning judicial personnel, rules of procedure, and the faulty administration of the business of the courts. This does not at all signify, however, that the substantive law is all that it should be. Far from it; on the contrary, once the immediate objectives we have been considering have been achieved, the really great task of jurisprudence in the second half of the twentieth century is to reform our substantive law to meet the needs of the times. Any judge or lawyer will recognize this fact if he will lift his eye from the microscope through which he has been studying individual cases and use a telescope to look at the law as a whole, as he must if he is truly interested in justice and in the law as an institution. This task, it must be admitted at the outset, is as difficult as the other three we have been discussing should prove easy.

Our civilization has passed through successive economic stages in which hunting and fishing, cattle raising and agriculture, exploration and mining, commerce and manufacturing, science, technology and mass production have predominated, until we have come today to the atomic age; therefore our law must, while still taking cognizance of the requirements of each of these eras of which none has been entirely superseded, be brought abreast of the demands of the age in which we live. For example, I had scarcely gone on the bench in the second most industrialized state of the Union [1] when we were called upon to decide between the conflicting claims of hunters and their dogs on the one hand and sheepraisers and their flocks on the other.[2] But another question to be faced was the extent of the right of a property owner in the air space above the ground he owns, which has only recently become a legal problem with the rapid increase in air transportation. In the early seventeenth century Coke could say without contradiction *"cujus est solum ejus est usque ad coelum"* [3] (whose is the soil, his it is up to the sky) but if this rule were applied today,

---

[1] Rhode Island is the most industrialized state.

[2] *Bunn v. Shaw*, 3 N.J. 195 (1949).

[3] Co. Litt. 4a.

airplane travel would be a very great source of litigation. Accordingly the courts in recent years have had
to readjust the respective rights of all concerned in the
light of one of the great facts of our scientific age. This
capacity of our law for growth, in large part by judicial
decision, is well recognized as one of the great virtues of
the common law, but the corresponding necessity for
pruning away dead or undesirable growth in the law
from time to time to meet the necessities of new conditions has not been so generally recognized. Both functions are essential and must be attended to with professional skill if the substantive law is to meet the manifold requirements of a complicated civilization. Dissatisfaction must inescapably result if the law fails to
keep pace with economic, scientific, political, and social
changes.

One inevitable result of this process of growth in the
law to meet the requirements of successive ages is the
enormous number of judicial decisions that reflect the
common law. The number of reported American decisions today has been estimated at 2,100,000, a number
to be compared with the 5,000 cases available to Coke
and Bacon in 1600 and the 10,000 decisions to be found
in the books in the time of Mansfield and Blackstone
150 years later. What is more, the number of reported
American decisions is increasing at the rate of 22,000
a month.[4] Obviously it is beyond the power of any finite
mind to read, let alone remember, all these decisions.

[4] Letter of Harvey T. Reid, President, West Publishing Co.,
Jan. 20, 1955.

More discouraging still to the litigant and his lawyer is the bulk of our legislation. In 1952–1953 the Congress and our state legislatures enacted 29,938 statutes,[5] and these merely supplemented the existing statutory compilations that filled 931 bulky volumes.

The volume of our administrative regulations is even more appalling. To check all of the federal administrative regulations one must search the 41 volumes of the Code of Federal Regulations of 1949 containing 22,055 pages and its annual pocket parts, as well as the current Federal Register, which in 1954 alone contained 9,910 pages. These figures for federal administrative regulations, moreover, are exclusive of specific legislation, such as is common in rate making and in banking matters, and of administrative interpretations of particular cases, none of which appear in the Federal Register and which are often very extensive.

When we turn from federal administrative regulations to federal administrative decisions, we may not even hazard a guess as to their magnitude, for many of them are never reported, but year by year the reported decisions of four agencies alone—the Bureau of Internal Revenue, the Tax Court of the United States, the National Labor Relations Board, and the Interstate Commerce Commission—approximate in volume the reports of all the federal courts of appeal and district courts!

Furthermore the bulk of state administrative law, both regulations and decisions, is largely unpublished. The states generally do not have anything comparable

[5] *The Book of the States* (*1954–1955*), pp. 112–113.

to the Federal Register, although fourteen of them do require some kind of publication of administrative regulations. Relatively few administrative decisions are published, however, and when they are, they generally appear in the much delayed annual reports of the state administrative agencies—too late to be of any real use.

Nor is most of our written law indexed at all or, if it is, the task is for the most part done inadequately. Accordingly, to the burden of intolerable bulk must be added the vice of unknowability in the vast wilderness of statutes and the jungle of administrative law.[6] We can find our way around, after a fashion at least, in the field of judicial decisions, with the aid of the digests, the encyclopedias, the textbooks, and the law reviews, but we have no such aids in the realm of legislation and administrative law. In fact we do not even have a uni-

---

[6] The problem is not confined to this country. The English situation is equally troublesome: "Still more remarkable is the fact that even lawyers themselves are quite inadequately acquainted with the system which they profess. Except as regards its more elementary provisions they are largely in the dark. This of course is by no means their fault. No human mind is sufficiently powerful to grasp the whole law as it now exists. Few indeed are able to achieve the mastery of any considerable department. English civil law, as an entire systm, is unknowable. 'By the great body of the legal profession (when engaged in advising those who resort to them for counsel), the law (generally speaking) is divined rather than ascertained; and whoever has seen opinions, even of celebrated lawyers, must know that they are often worded with a discreet and studied ambiguity, which, while it saves the credit of the uncertain and perplexed adviser, thickens the doubts of the party who is seeking instruction and guidance.' " Hart, *The Way to Justice*, p. 14 (1941).

form, not to mention a scientific, scheme of indexing statutes and administrative regulations and decisions. Nor has it been possible to interest any publisher or foundation in such a project despite persistent efforts in that direction. Professor Frederic J. Stimson's *American Statute Law,* published in 1886, is the latest effort to summarize our statute law. The famous case of *Panama Refining Company v. Ryan* is an outstanding instance of the inaccessibility of our modern materials in the field of written law. That case reached the Supreme Court of the United States on the false assumption that a section of the Petroleum Code contained a paragraph which, in fact, had long since been deleted by executive order. Chief Justice Hughes complained:

> "Whatever the cause of the failure to give appropriate public notice of the change in the section, with the result that the person affected, the prosecuting authorities, and the courts, were alike ignorant of the alteration, the fact is that the attack in this respect was upon a provision which did not exist." [7]

Not only is the volume of our law overwhelming, not only is much of it inaccessible, but much of our statute law and our administrative law is of an inferior quality

[7] 293 U.S. 388, at 412, 55 S. Ct. 241, at 245, 79 L. ed. 446, at 454 (1935). See also Griswold, "Government in Ignorance of the Law—A Plea for Better Publication of Executive Legislation," 48 *Harv. L. Rev.* 198 (1934); Jaffe: "Publication of Administrative Rules and Orders," 24 *A.B.A.J.* 393 (1938); Ronald, "Publication of Federal Administrative Legislation," 7 *Geo. Wash. L. Rev.* 52 (1938).

from the standpoint of draftsmanship as well as of substance. This also is bound to cause difficulties and dissatisfaction in the adaptation of the law to modern requirements.

But even if the quality of our legal pronouncements
were what it should be, and even if its volume were not
so tremendous and so inaccessible, we would still be con-
fronted with the underlying fact that our law speaks
from various eras and that the objectives of one era
often are in conflict with those of another era, and that
therefore our law not only lacks consistency and har-
mony but is not adapted to modern needs. This has
led to an increase in demand in certain quarters for total
codification; but that, I submit, is alien to our traditional modes of legal thinking. But whatever its form
may be—and of that I shall speak later—we impera-
tively require a modernization of the law adapted to the
needs of our rapidly changing times before the law
breaks down of its own weight.

This is not the first time that the legal profession has
been called upon to adapt the law to the needs of a new
era in a time of crisis. In the reign of Charles I it took
a revolution to enable Lord Coke and the other parliamentary leaders of his time to overcome the Stuart
heresy of the divine right of kings and to curb the royal
prerogative. In doing so they not only preserved but
strengthened the doctrine of the supremacy of law and
warded off the reception of the Roman law in England
by destroying the Star Chamber and regularizing the
practice of Chancery. The struggle, as Maitland takes

pains to point out in his Rede lecture,[8] was not a placid encounter of disembodied ideas, but the fierce struggle of leaders of the Inns of Court, the law schools of that day, in Parliament and in the courts to preserve the essentials of their native law. Again, in the troubled period of the Industrial Revolution, the American Revolution, and the French Revolution, the transition to a new economic, political, and social age was ably guided by the leaders of the bench and bar. Mansfield and Hardwicke, Burke, Blackstone and Bentham in England, and in this country Hamilton and Jefferson, Jay and Madison, Kent and Story, the framers of the Federal Constitution, and the painstaking draftsmen in the several states who laboriously adapted the statutes of England to the needs of new commonwealths, once more preserved the essentials of our traditional law and liberty while adapting it to the spirit of a new era. But in the period of the Jacksonian Revolution, as we have seen, when equality in fact as distinguished from the Jeffersonian equality of opportunity was the grand objective, the bench found itself under attack and the bar seemingly had lost its capacity for sagacious leadership. The bar of that day failed both the profession and the public miserably. The result was a lowering of judicial and professional standards, a lessening of respect for the courts and the law, and the failure of the law to keep pace with economic and social changes.

Now we are living in another era of rapid change. Indeed it is beyond any doubt that the velocity of change

[8] Maitland, *English Law and the Renaissance* (1901).

in our civilization at the present time is greater than in any previous era of the common law. This has resulted not only from the application of scientific and engineering inventions and discoveries, but from world wars, the clash of political ideologies and of Eastern and Western civilizations. The only other period at all comparable to ours in these respects is the era which included the American Revolution, the French Revolution, and the Industrial Revolution. The law then met and encompassed the startling political, economic, and social changes that were occurring. Lawyers, judges, and statesmen then sought out all knowledge and wisdom that was available to them from the past or from their contemporaries and applied it to the solution of the great problems of the day. Witness Madison ransacking the pages of history and political science in preparation for the work of the Constitutional Convention. Witness Kent, despising the French Revolution but quoting French jurists to buttress his efforts to adapt the common law to the needs of a young country, and to popularize the system of equity that the people of many states frowned upon, largely because the chancellor acted without the aid of a jury. Witness Mansfield, removing the barnacles from the legal procedure of his day, adapting old forms of action to new ends of justice and bringing the law merchant of continental Europe within the scope of the common law.

What lawyers have done before they can and will do again. The conditions confronting us today, however, are vastly more involved than those of a century and a half ago. They cast a heavy burden on the profession which we can and will meet. We must quicken our pace and raise our standards. We must cover all and not a mere part of the field that is ours to defend. At the same time we must keep our balance, our sense of proportion. Like Madison and Kent and Mansfield, we must use precedents and contemporaneous experience—and our own common sense. We must imbue our students with the belief that they are to be the physicians, the architects, and the engineers of the social order. We must inspire them to be intellectually alert and open-minded, to be tolerant of everything except wrong. As Professor John Hazard, speaking recently on the "Contrasting Principles in Soviet and Common Law," has said: "The common law prepares the way for the effective competition of ideas in the expectation that out of the conflict will emerge a flexible way of life which will benefit us all." [9]

Our responsibilities today are not only national but international, and in international affairs we are unprepared emotionally as well as intellectually. While the dangers are recognized by some, as a profession and as a people we still seem quite unaware of the dangers inherent in the basic conflict between rapidly expanding governmental activities in an age of tension and our cherished traditions of individual liberty. Individual liberty may well shrink drastically or even perish in an

[9] U. of Chicago Law School Conference on Jurisprudence and Politics 20, at 29. No. 15, April 30, 1954.

age of fear, but with forethought, skill, and courage the needs both of government and of individual liberty may be served. Impending changes may be intelligent, based on all the available facts in a changing social order and grounded on a true insight into the virtues as well as the infirmities of human nature, or they may be haphazard and unthinking. It is for us to choose whether we will follow the example of the leaders of the bench and bar in the Stuart period and in the era of the three revolutions, or surrender to irresponsible change as in the Jacksonian period. In the last half-century the organized bar has gone far to redeem the profession from the stigma of defaults of a century ago; it has led the way in formulating the canons of professional and judicial ethics and in policing their enforcement, in promoting sound standards of legal education, of judicial administration and of administrative procedure, and in agitating for the exercise by the Federal courts of the rule-making power.

But the task we are now contemplating is of far greater magnitude than any undertaken in the past by the legal profession in any common-law country. To whom shall we turn for help? What instrumentalities have we available for this tremendous task? Manifestly we cannot expect the judges of today to duplicate the great work of Glanvil and Bracton, Littleton and Fortescue, Bacon and Coke, Hale and Blackstone, who not only epitomized the law of the age in which they lived, but by so doing prepared the way for needed im-

provements. In the work of these great jurists, as Holdsworth has demonstrated,[10] may be found the charts of
the great currents of English law for centuries. Much
the same thing may be said for the work of Kent and
Story in this country. But clearly we may not expect our
leading judges, hard pressed as they are, to keep abreast
of their judicial work and also to head up the work of
law reform in the grand manner, though they can render
indispensable service by way of advice and criticism.
The capable, practicing lawyers of today are likewise
far too busy to give us leadership in the movement for
law reform as Edward Livingston and David Dudley
Field did in their day, though in every age there may be
found a few lawyers whose help would likewise be invaluable.

If we may not look to judges or lawyers for leadership
in law reform, to whom may we turn? Some of the best
minds of the English bench and bar have struggled for
over a century for a ministry of justice as an instru-
mentality of law reform. They envision a public official
of high cabinet rank who shall devote himself and his
department to the great task of law reform and the
administration of the law. Lord Langdell, Master of the
Rolls, in 1836,[11] Lord Chancellor Westbury in 1857,[12]
Lord Chancellor Haldane in 1918,[13] all espoused the
idea of a ministry of justice in eloquent words, but with

[10] Holdsworth, *Some Makers of English Law* (1938).
[11] Hansard, 3d series, vol. 34, at 447–450.
[12] Nash, *Life of Lord Westbury,* vol. 1, at 190.
[13] See Sixth Report and Evidence (Cd. 7832 and 8130).

little success. The movement has its lesson for us. Because the English have no constitutional doctrine of separation of powers such as we have, seemingly their problem of law reform should be easily solved by an official body. They have, moreover, a mere 350,000 decisions to deal with, compared with our millions, and their statutes and administrative regulations are fewer in number and concededly more skillfully drawn than ours in many jurisdictions. Nor does anyone venture to question the character, independence, or competence of the English judges, whatever else they may complain of with respect to the judicial system. Not only is the English problem simpler than ours, but at the same time their need is greater by reason of the stalemate resulting from the strict English version of the doctrine of *stare decisis* and the practical impossibility of obtaining parliamentary time for presenting curative bills to overcome the effect of undesirable judicial decisions. It was the misfortune of English law that its doctrine of judicial infallibility was being extended to the ultimate (in an age when science was freely discarding its prior misconceptions) at a time when the only available remedy—legislation in Parliament—was being practically eliminated by the pressure of government measures on available legislative time. We must not be misled by the success of an occasional private bill such as Sir A. P. Herbert's Matrimonial Causes Act of 1938. Although the government for political reasons did not desire to sponsor the bill, it nevertheless recognized the necessity for it and did not impede its enactment.

Occasionally to be sure, some major work of law reform has been taken up by the government. Thus in 1894 F. E. Smith obtained a first class grade at Oxford when he took the Honours School of Jurisprudence examination, but the next year when he took the B.C.L. examination he gave the wrong answer to a question on the *Rule in Shelley's case,* with the result that he received only a second class grade. He vowed that "When I am Lord Chancellor I shall abolish that rule!"—and exactly thirty years later he did just that in the course of modernizing the real property law of England in the legislation that popularly bears his name.[14] But there have been few F. E. Smith's at the bar and even fewer Lord Chancellors like Lord Birkenhead, and even Birkenhead relied largely on the knowledge of a group of experts who had been working in this field for years.

The opponents of a ministry of justice have been equally distinguished—Lord Chancellor Birkenhead; [15] Lord Chief Justice Hewart; [16] Lord Schuster,[17] long Permanent Secretary to the Lord Chancellor; Sir Arthur L. Goodhart,[18] the distinguished editor of the Law Quarterly Review—and they have assigned many reasons for their opposition, but it remained for an

[14] Goodhart, "Law Reform," address broadcast in the Third Programme of the British Broadcasting Corporation (1952).

[15] Birkenhead, *Points of View,* vol. 1, pp. 108–109 (1922).

[16] Hewart, *The New Despotism,* pp. 110–111 (1929).

[17] Schuster, "Problems of Legal Administration," II *Politica* 239 (1937).

[18] Address entitled "Law Reform" delivered before the Holdsworth Club on March 7, 1952.

American student of comparative law, Henry Selden Bacon, to state openly what seems to be the underlying fear on the part of many English judges and lawyers. He labels the movement for the adoption of a ministry of justice on the continental model as an "effort to impair human rights by enfeebling the courts." [19] He points out that although on the surface one would suppose that the French judiciary is independent, this is not true in fact due to the powers exercised by the French Ministry of Justice which are termed "so extraordinary . . . and openly or covertly used by it that a bare statement of them could hardly be made plausible without first giving some idea of the curiously ductile medium in which these powers work." [20] The French Ministry of Justice has amazing powers: in every civil and criminal court the ministry has a representative who has an absolute right to be heard in every case and in some courts to be present in secret deliberations of the judges; the representative may command any judge to come to his office and give explanations as to "any acts which may be imputed to him"; the representative wears a judicial robe, has a judicial bench of his own and is paid a salary equal to that of the president of the court (no judge may criticize him even for misconduct in open court); it is largely on the recommendation of this representative that the promotion of judges is made. To

[19] Bacon, "On a Ministry of Justice," 22 *Va. L. Rev.* 175 (1935).

[20] ibid., 176. Cf. Edwards, "The Ministry of Justice in France," 8 *N.C.L. Rev.* 328 (1930).

illustrate the power of this representative Bacon points out that in one year the highest court in France, the Court of Cassation, approved and followed the conclusions submitted by the Ministry's representative in 97½% of the cases before it. He characterizes the French judge as "a functionary in the same sense as is the policeman or the fireman, and like them . . . subject with regard to all his acts, to 'discipline' at the hands of his superiors." [21] He states:

> "The record illustrates one difference between French ideas of judicial independence and those which have prevailed in countries of the common law since 1689, and clearly throws upon the advocate of the introduction of such a Ministry and the admirers of the judicial method of the civilians the burden of showing that a French judgment in general is in fact a judicial and not an executive determination." [22]

How much of this thinking is in the minds of English judges and lawyers and the public in considering a ministry of justice is impossible for an American to say.[23] With these thoughts in mind we can better understand Lord Schuster's observations:

> "The police, generally speaking, are popular in this country; but . . . horror of a police state is deep and strong, and rests very largely (though wholly

[21] *op. cit.*, 185.

[22] ibid., 185.

[23] See, however, DeMontmorency, "Do We Need a Ministry of Justice," 181 *Contemporary Rev.* 233, pp. 235–236 (April 1952).

unconsciously) on the idea that a close union between the executive and judicial power must result in tyranny." [24]

The thoughts expressed by Bacon and Lord Schuster are so foreign to our Anglo-American concept of judicial independence (except as marred in practice in such jurisdictions here, where politics intrude by reason of the necessities of judicial elections) as to be almost unbelievable. If the reader has any doubts as to the position of the judge in the continental system, they will be dispelled by the measured words of one of the greatest of Italian jurists, Piero Calamandrei, in writing of his own courts:

"In the parliamentary democracy, the Parliament which represents the sovereign people exercises a sovereign political control over the whole of the governmental activity; and each of the ministers responds before the Parliament (principle of 'ministerial responsibility') for the good functioning of that branch of the public administration of which he is the head; and to remain in his position he has need of the Parliament's confidence.

"Even the administration of justice is a branch of the public administration, at the head of which stands the Minister of Justice, who as every other Minister

[24] Schuster, "The Office of the Lord Chancellor," 10 *Cambridge L.J.* 175, p. 190 (1949). See also for his historical summary, Gardiner, "The Machinery of Law Reform in England," 69 *L.Q. Rev.* 46 (1953).

for his own department, answers before the Parliament for the good functioning of the judicial organs. But to answer for their good functioning it is necessary that he have the organizing and disciplinary powers indispensable to maintain it or to augment its efficiency in a manner corresponding to the exigencies of the service; to correct inconveniences, to repress abuses it is requisite, therefore, that the Minister have an effective superintendence (*ingerenza*) over the activity and the discipline of the judicial organs. But this power in relation to the judiciary necessarily signifies dependence of the judges on the Minister.

"The principle of the independence of the judiciary, of the judiciary as 'an order autonomous and independent of every other power,' thus remains, so long as this system prevails, a purely platonic expression. The magistracy, understood as a judicial organization, is not autonomous, because, constituting one of the branches of public administration, it depends on the Minister of Justice who is head of this branch, and through the Minister on the Government.

"There is thus in this hybrid system a contradiction between two principles, which is concretely reflected in the individual discomfort of every judge. It is true that the judge at the moment when he decides is the organ of a sovereign function, who does not receive orders from any superior; but it is also true that the same judge, to be able to exercise this function, has been appointed by the State in the quality of a public employee, bound to the public administration by a relation of retributed labor, with the right to a salary, and with corresponding duties of office. . . .

"The danger of this hybrid system is evident. The Minister, who is a political organ, can be tempted, on the occasion of some case which has political importance, to avail himself of the hierarchical superintendence which he has over the administrative position (the so-called 'career') and the discipline of the employee, in order to bring about deviation from or to limit in fact the independence of the judge. It is true that as judge the magistrate is free juridically to decide as his conscience dictates; but if the Minister, or the politicians who lurk in his shadow, should discreetly give him to understand that upon the manner in which he will decide a certain case may depend a desired promotion or a distasteful transfer, it is easy to see how in this way there may go to work on the conscience of the judge those disturbing stimuli of private order, in which the employee, who thinks of his salary and of the education of his children cannot remain insensible. . . ."[25]

The author goes on to speak of the effort to remedy these difficulties through the establishment of a "Superior Council of the Magistracy." It appeared, however,

[25] Piero Calamandrei, *Processo e Democrazia* (in process of translation by Professor John Clark Adams of the University of Beirut, to be published in the near future by the Institute of Comparative Law of New York University). I am indebted to Professor Robert Wyness Millar of Northwestern University School of Law for calling this work to my attention and for supplying me with the foregoing translation.

that the implementing law was still under discussion at the time of the lecture. And in any case Calamandrei thinks that the individual independence of the judge would still be lacking as long as he retains the quality of a public employee "who lives on his salary and is naturally desirous of promotion and economic betterment."

Though a ministry of justice has been advocated by some of our ablest jurists, such as Dean Pound and Justice Cardozo, we may not hope for the institution of a program of law reform through any official body in a country as devoted as this country is to the doctrine of the separation of powers and where—equally important—the executive and legislative branches and often the judicial branches of government work in an atmosphere of suspicion of each other if not of outright antagonism.[26]

Nor can we turn to our law schools as presently oriented. Their primary aim has been the education of

[26] 22 *Am. J. of Soc.* 721 (May 1917); "Anachronisms in Law," 3 *J. Am. Jud. Soc.* 142, pp. 143 (Feb. 1920). Cardozo ,"A Ministry of Justice," 35 *Harv. L. Rev.* 112, at 113–114 (1921). The single exception to this statement of which I am aware is the Louisiana State Law Institute founded in 1938 (La. Act 166 of 1938 now La. R. S. 24:201–204) which is an official advisory law reform commission, law reform agency, and legal research agency of the State of Louisiana, composed of judges, legislators, practising lawyers, and law teachers from the three law schools. Ferdinand F. Stone, "The Louisiana State Law Institute," 4 *The American Journal of Comparative Law,* p. 85 (1955).

the oncoming generation of the profession, but there are various parts of that task for which they have not yet generally assumed responsibility, such as the teaching of law in the light of present-day economic, political, and social facts and trends, training in the fundamental skills of an attorney, education in the arts of the advocate, the inculcation of an awareness of the perplexing problems of professional and judicial ethics and of responsibility for the improvement of law and of the administration of justice and for leadership in public affairs. Yet in spite of all of the admitted shortcomings of legal education today, I doubt if any other students in America work harder or more enthusiastically or more profitably than our first- and second-year law students. One of the great satisfactions of teaching law, indeed for many the greatest satisfaction, is in helping young minds catch fire intellectually for the first time through the study in the Socratic tradition of the law in action.

But whatever the shortcomings of legal education, it is still to the law school faculties that we must turn for the core of the work of law reform. They have an accumulation of specialized legal knowledge, at least of the substantive law as found in the books, that is available nowhere else, and they have the best available environment for undertaking such a task. Individual professors have long made their contributions to improving the law. What is needed is entire faculties dedicated to that end. Any law school which lifts its sights beyond the traditional role of training law students and faces the problem of law reform is properly called a law center. It is to such law centers that we must turn for the performance, at least in the substantive field of the law, of what is clearly the great task of the law school in the second half of the twentieth century.

The modernization of the law calls for help, as I have already said, from judges and lawyers who have the knowledge, experience, and wisdom to give it. Our law centers should be the meeting places of legal scholars of all kinds. We should go further. We should welcome the cooperation of laymen who are interested in the law. The layman can ask questions that will jar the complacency of the legal mind. It is not a mere coincidence that the most useful judicial councils and conferences in this country are those including lay members. We need laymen to remind us occasionally that the law is not the only angle from which to view life, that law is not the only means of maintaining the social order and of promoting individual welfare. At the same time, we need to have the expert come to us from the bench, from the forum, and from the administrator's conference table to bring us the distillation of his ripe experience and seasoned wisdom. There is nothing new about all this; it was, in essence, the way in which the law saved itself in the past. We must gather together in law centers the most thoughtful and experienced of our judges, legislators, law school professors, social scientists, and especially businessmen from all walks of life, representing industry, labor, and the ordinary citizen and put them to work around a conference table where they can bring their varied experience and mature judgment to the solution of vital legal problems in the public interest.[27]

This is the method we have traditionally employed in our constitutional conventions. The Advisory Committees of the United States Supreme Court that drafted the Federal Rules of Civil and Criminal Procedure owe much of their success to the variety of the experience, both professional and geographic, of their members, as well as to the innumerable state and local committees and individuals they consulted. And in England Lord Mansfield habitually consulted businessmen on questions of the law merchant; some of them, according to Lord Campbell, became almost professional jurors in his court.

I am not suggesting that any one law center attempt to cover the entire field of American law, but the law schools of each state have a special responsibility for improving the law of their own state. Such a task will serve to break down the wall that in too many states has isolated the law schools from the bar, to the great loss of both. This work will naturally start with an exposi-

[27] Dean Pound put it well in his "A Ministry of Justice; A New Role for the Law School", 38 *A.B.A. Journal* 637, p. 705 (1952). Tiring of waiting for the creation of an official agency for law reform, he here took the advanced position that "a duty is cast upon the faculty of the law school of a state university, both as members of the teaching profession and as members of the legal profession, to exercise the learned arts they pursue in the spirit of a public service in the great and needed service of taking upon themselves the role of a Ministry of Justice."

tion of the existing law of the state. In some states there are already annual surveys of state law which render an invaluable service to the bench and bar of the state, systematically helping them keep abreast of current developments in state law. Some law schools will, it is to be hoped, attempt to cover parts of the field on a national or international scale. There is no reason why groups of law schools may not cooperate not only to their own advantage but to the benefit of everyone concerned with the law. The recently organized American Bar Research Center is in a position to provide leadership for the entire movement. Its current progress for the study of the criminal law and its enforcement on a national basis is an example of what may be done in many fields.

The first step on both state and national law will necessarily be to ascertain what the law is and how it attained its present form. Here, surprisingly, the number of great textbooks has been far less in the first half of the twentieth century than it was in the first half of the nineteenth. Recently I queried three distinguished professors of law and one outstanding law librarian for the names of the great law books that had been published in the first half of the twentieth century by law professors. I wanted not books projected, but actually published—other books comparable to Williston or Corbin on Contracts, Scott or Bogert on Trusts, or Wigmore on Evidence and Pound's voluminous writings. In each case the answer came back, "The great law books of the first half of the twentieth century are Williston and Cor-

bin, Scott and Bogert, Wigmore and Pound." The great
textbooks of the first half of the nineteenth century not
only outnumbered the great textbooks of the first half of
the twentieth century—Kent's Commentaries (1826–
1830); Gould on Pleading (1832); Story on Bailments
(1832), on the Constitution (1833), on the Conflict of
Laws (1834,) on Equity Jurisprudence (1836), on
Equity Pleading (1838), on Agency (1839), on Part-
nership (1841), on Bills of Exchange (1843), on Prom-
issory Notes (1845); Wheaton on International Law
(1836); Greenleaf on Evidence (1842–1853); Whar-
ton on Criminal Law (1846); Sedgwick on Damages
(1847) and on Interpretation of Statutory and Constitutional Law (1857); Rawle on Covenants for Title
(1852); Bishop on Marriage and Divorce (1852) and
on Criminal Law (1856–1858); Parsons on Contracts
(1853–1855); Washburn on Real Property (1860–
1862) [28]—but, except for the six modern authors we
have mentioned, far exceeded them in influence. And yet
the need of great textbooks is even greater than when
Dean Ames wrote over forty years ago:

> "From the nature of the case the judge cannot be ex-
> pected to engage in original historical investigations,
> nor can he approach the case before him from the
> point of view of one who has made a minute and com-
> prehensive examination of the branch of the law of
> which the question to be decided forms a part. The
> judge is not and ought not to be a specialist. But it

[28] Pound, *The Formative Era in American Law* 140–141 (1938).

is his right, of which he has too long been deprived, to have the benefit of the conclusions of specialists or professors, whose writings represent years of study and reflection, and are illuminated by the light of history, analysis, and the comparison of the laws of different countries. The judge may or may not accept the conclusions of the professor, as he may accept or reject the arguments of counsel. But that the treatises of the professors will be of a quality to render invaluable service to the judge and that they are destined to exercise a great influence in the further development of our law, must be clear to every thoughtful lawyer." [29]

Unfortunately for our present purposes, too much of our legal scholarship has gone into the editing of casebooks. These casebooks are invaluable for the law student—they are the means of teaching him how to mine for the pure gold of legal principles—but they have not given judges or practicing lawyers the help which Dean Ames fairly said they are entitled to get. An encyclopedia can never take the place of a well-executed text which embodies a lifetime of experience and study. Great textbooks are as essential as ever in the development of the law, and obviously increasing attention must be given to their preparation as part of the process of understanding the law.

But it may be urged, are not the various volumes of the *Restatement of the Law* adequate to meeting the de-

[29] Ames, *Lectures on Legal History* 367 (1913).

mands of the times for the simplification of the law? Can we not be spared the tremendous burden which such a task of preparing exhaustive textbooks would impose on us? It would be comfortable, indeed, to be able to answer this question in the affirmative, especially in view of the indebtedness of every judge and lawyer to the *Restatement,* but unfortunately the *Restatement* will not serve our necessities. The Code of Hammurabi, the Code of Justinian, and the Code Napoléon each summarized authoritatively the law of a great empire. Although the *Restatement* partakes of the form of a code,[30] thereby arousing the antipathy that all statutes, and codes in particular, call forth in the mind of the average American lawyer, it is not a code and it does not have the force of statutes.[31] The *Restatement,* indeed, has very little to do with statutes and nothing at all to do with administrative law, but is concerned almost exclusively with judge-made law.[32] Nevertheless,

[30] Lewis: "The Work of the American Law Institute," 9 *American Law School Rev.* 724 (1939).

[31] "We are not seeking to formulate a code of law for enactment by the legislatures." 2 *Proceedings A.L.I.* 21 (1924). See Yntema, "The American Law Institute" in *Legal Essays . . . to Orrin McMurray* (1935), 657, 673; Havighurst, "Restatement of the Law of Contracts," 27 *Ill. L. Rev.* 910, 919 (1933); but cf. Franklin: "The Historic Function of the American Law Institute," 47 *Harv. L. Rev.* 1367 (1934).

[32] See 2 *Proceedings A.L.I.* 50 (1924). The purpose of the formation of the American Law Institute was reiterated to be the preservation of the common law by Dr. Lewis, the director, in "Present Status of the American Law Institute," 6 *New York University Law Quarterly Review* 337 (1929); cf. Perkins, "What Would Law Teachers Like to See the Institute Do," 8 *Am. L.*

unlike our judicial decisions, the *Restatement* does not state what we consider the essence of decisions, the reasons for the rule of law laid down.[33] It does not even cite cases and statutes as does, for example, Jenks' *Digest of English Civil Law*.[34] Nor does the *Restatement* purport to set forth the common law of every state; rather it relies on state annotations to give such aid to the bench and bar in each jurisdiction.[35] These annotations, however, are not available for every state and every subject. They are, moreover, separate documents for each state, which do not provide in any one place an over-all picture of the law of our forty-nine jurisdictions; consequently there is no easy method of determining whether a given proposition in any of the

---

Sch. Rev. 498 (1935); Yntema, "What Should the American Law Institute Do?" 34 *Michigan Law Review* 461, 465 (1936).

[33] As originally conceived, it was intended that the Restatement include "the reason for the law as it is." 1 *Proceedings A.L.I.* Part I, at 14, Organizing Committee Report (1923). But cf. Arnold, "Institute Priests and Yale Observers," 84 *U. Pa. L. Rev.* 811 (1936); Lorenzo and Heilman, "The Restatement of the Conflict of Laws," 83 *U. Pa. L. Rev.* 555, 585 (1935); Patterson, "Restatement of the Law of Contracts," 33 *Col. L. Rev.* 397, 401, 426 (1933); Wright, "The American Law Institute Restatements of Contracts and Agency," 1 *Toronto Law Journal* 15, 29 (1935); Yntema, *op. cit.*, note 31, at 672.

[34] This treatise was published with the announced profession "merely to state the rules which are covered by existing authority," but in contrast to the *Restatement*, "authority has been quoted for substantially every rule stated in the text of the work." *Digest of English Civil Law* (Jenks, 2nd ed. 1921), iii, v. See also the current edition, Prolegomena and Preface (Winfield, Bailey, Lewis, Latey, Orr, Thomas, ed., 1948).

[35] *Restatement in the Courts* (1945), 12.

Restatements represents the law in all of the states or simply in a majority or minority of jurisdictions, or merely the view, possibly the divided view, of the Institute.[36]

The *Restatement* does not concern itself with any of the subjects of public law nor with the vexing problems of procedural law and judicial administration, except for its Code of Criminal Procedure and its Model Code of Evidence, which have in effect been superseded by the Uniform Rules of Criminal Procedure and the Uniform Rules of Evidence. The *Restatement* thus reflects the preoccupation of the profession with private substantive law. But it does not even cover the field of substantive law with completeness, partnerships, corporations, family, and divorce law being omitted along with other important subjects. Nor is it intended to be either a commentary on the subjects covered or a history of them, although the Institute originally intended that treatises should accompany the individual restatements.[37] It purports merely to constitute a new starting-point out of the welter of decisions for such subjects of our private substantive law as it treats: Agency, Con-

[36] Lewis, "The Work of the American Law Institute," 9 *Am. L. Sch. Rev.* 724, 725 (1939); cf. Clark, "Restatement of the Law of Contracts," 42 *Yale L.J.* 656–60 (1933). See also remarks of Karl Llewellyn, *Proceedings,* American Bar Association, Judicial Section 43–6 (Milwaukee, August 28, 1934).

[37] Lewis, "The American Law Institute and Its Work," 24 *Col. L. Rev.* 621, 626 (1924). The plan to have treatises accompany the *Restatement* was abandoned at an early date. *Restatement in the Courts* (1945) 8; cf. 3 *Proceedings A.L.I.* 409, 416 (1925).

flict of Laws, Contracts, Judgments, Property, Restitution, Security, Torts, and Trusts.[38]

The *Restatement* aspires to be more than merely another expression of the law.[39] It aims to achieve an authority much higher than an ordinary treatise, its authority being predicated, however, not on any reasoning set forth therein, but rather on the standing of its draftsmen and their advisers and the Council of the Institute.[40] It is conceded, however, that any particular proposition in the *Restatement* may not be supported by the weight of authority or even the unanimous opinion of the reporter and his advisers or of the Council of the Institute,[41] and it is impossible to ascertain from the *Restatement* on what authority each proposition is based. Nevertheless, in the language of its director, Dr. William Draper Lewis, it was expected from the beginning that the *Restatement* "will result in giving its

[38] 2 *Proceedings A.L.I.* 21–2 (1924); Madden, "The American Law Institute," 29 *West Virginia Law Quarterly* 149 (1923); Wickersham, "The American Law Institute and the Projected Restatement of the Common Law in America," 43 *Law Quarterly Review* 449, 489 (1927); cf. Hicks, *Materials and Methods of Legal Research* (3rd ed., 1942). pp. 191, 194.

[39] 2 *Proceedings A.L.I.* 36, 50 (1924).

[40] 2 *ibid.*, p. 21; *Restatement in the Courts* (1945) 9; Lewis, "Present Status of the American Law Institute," 6 *N.Y.U.L.Q. Rev.* 337, 341 (1929).

[41] See various critics: Clark, note 36, supra; Corbin, "Restatement of the Common Law," 15 *Iowa Law Review* 19 (1929); Patterson, "Restatement of the Law of Contracts," 33 *Col. L. Rev.* 397, 402, 426 (1933); Bingham, "The American Law Institute vs. The Supreme Court, In the Matter of Haddock v. Haddock," 21 *Corn. L. Q.* 393, 423 (1936).

statement of the rules of law a position of prima facie authority as to what the common law is." [42]

At its inception in 1923 the Institute aimed, among other things, "to promote the clarification and simplification of the law and its better adaptation to social needs . . . ," [43] but the third objective of the better adaptation of the law to social needs was soon subordinated to promoting clarification and simplification of the law because of the difficulty of reconciling the obvious conflict in objectives.[44] As Chief Justice Hughes put it at an annual meeting of the American Law Institute, "We must not lose sight of the great objective. The quest of certainty may be endless and the goal may be unattainable, but progress is practicable. Focusing attention on definite propositions, it [the *Restatement*] cannot fail to facilitate discussion and improvement." [45]

The original aspiration of the Institute for a systematic classification of the law as a basis for the *Restatement* [46] was soon forgotten in following the tra-

[42] *Proceedings,* American Bar Association, Judicial Section 10 (Milwaukee, August 28, 1934).

[43] See Report of Organizing Committee: 1 *Proceedings A.L.I.* Part I, p. 41 (1923); similarly see the Charter of the American Law Institute, *ibid.,* Part II, pp. 21, 33.

[44] See remarks of Lewis, *Proceedings* of the American Bar Association, Judicial Section, *op. cit.,* note 42, p. 9; Clark, *op. cit.,* note 36; Yntema, *op. cit.,* note 32.

[45] Hughes, "Address to American Law Institute, 10th Annual Meeting," 19 *A.B.A.J.* 325, 326 (1933). See also Goble, "Restatement of the Law of Contracts," 21 *California Law Review* 421 (1933).

[46] See Report of Organizing Committee, *op. cit.,* note 43, Part I, at 14, Part II at 46; also 2 *Proceedings A.L.I.* 28–32

ditional headings of our law; [47] the watertight compartments of the courses in the law schools dictated for the most part the divisions of subjects in the *Restatement*. The goal of scientific terminology was frustrated,[48] as so many times before in the history of the common law, by the unscientific and so-called practical mind of the profession; the Institute's director, William Draper Lewis, has said that the *Restatement* "has failed in more than one instance to carry out my expressed desire to use one word to state each fundamental legal concept and not to use any word to express more than one fundamental legal concept." [49] A golden opportunity for systematic classification and scientific precision in legal thinking was lost.

Although the aims of the American Law Institute

(1924). See Pound, *ibid.*, pp. 381–425; Salmond, "The Literature of the Law," 22 *Col. L. Rev.* 197 (1922), as to need for scientific classification. Criticism of the classification used in the *Restatement,* based as it is on the curriculum in the law school, was made by Franklin, "The Historic Function of the American Law Institute," 47 *Harv. L. Rev.* 1367–94 (1934). As to need for classification, see Arnold, *op. cit.,* note 33 supra.

[47] E.g., 1 *Proceedings A.L.I.* Part III at 62, 92 (1923); *Restatement in the Courts* (1945), 9. The work as engaged in was undertaken because law school professor-authorities were available.

[48] Farnum: "Terminology and the American Law Institute," 13 *Boston University Law Review* 203 (1933).

[49] 21 *Proceedings A.L.I.* 39 (1944). Thus it was said earlier: "By May, 1926, there had developed the fact that . . . the greatest difficulty in the production of any restatement of the law was . . . the selection of the terminology, at once clear and adequate . . . for the restatement of all subjects." 9 *ibid.* at 34 (1931).

have been universally hailed with approval, opinion has varied as to the merits of the *Restatement*. As early as 1927 Walter Wheeler Cook stated that the entire plan of the *Restatement* was of little value because its statements were too general to be of use, lacked references to authority, and failed to include explanations and reasoning.[50] He suggested an authoritative encyclopedia to absorb all textbooks and provide all necessary references to the decisions. Dean, now Chief Judge, Charles E. Clark has criticized the work as giving the public the dry pulp without the life-giving juices, the early plan for treatises explaining the *Restatement* having been abandoned.[51] He also attacked the idea of making one common law for the country and rejected the thought that a statement of the law could be written that would be useful throughout the land. He was concerned with the problem of restating the law where it depends on a statute or where the existing rule of law has died out, and he criticized the tendency to state the law as it ought to be under the guise of stating the law as it is. Others have lamented the failure to consider the momentum of social change or to compare our experience with that of foreign law.[52]

While the work of the American Law Institute as

[50] Cook, "Legal Research," 13 *A.B.A.J.* 281 (1927).

[51] Clark, *op. cit.*, note 36, p. 647.

[52] Corbin, *op. cit.*, note 41, p. 27; Havighurst, *op. cit.*, note 31, p. 915; Yntema, "The American Law Institute" in *Legal Essays . . . to Orrin McMurray* (1935), 657; Yntema, "What Should the American Law Institute Do?" 34 *Mich. L. Rev.* 461 (1936).

embodied in the *Restatement* has not achieved its original goal of supplanting the citation of cases,[53] it has been in constant use in the courts for years and it is difficult to imagine practicing law today without it. The Institute has compiled a formidable record of all the citations of the *Restatement* in reports and legal periodicals,[54] which attests the great advantage it has enjoyed of accessibility, an advantage that will continue to increase its prestige over the years. One of the great collateral benefits of the *Restatement* to the profession has been its stimulus to legal scholarship, manifested in textbooks, casebooks, and innumerable law review articles.[55] Opinion differs as to its effect on law teaching, some maintaining that it has taken the edge off the use of the case method, others claiming that it has greatly advanced the study of law as a system. It definitely serves to familiarize the student at an early point with the use of materials in the form of a code. Finally, the American Law Institute has rendered a great service to the profession by setting an example of cooperative endeavor, which has been followed in such enterprises as the drafting of the Federal Rules of Civil

[53] *2 Proceedings A.L.I.* 21 (1924).

[54] *Restatement in the Courts* (1945), iii, v. More than 10,000 citations in court decisions to January 1, 1945 are noted. See Ransom, Book Review, *32 A.B.A.J.* 188 (1946). Cf. Hicks, *op. cit.*, note 38, supra.

[55] 13 *Proceedings A.L.I.* 85 (1936); see Clark, *op. cit.*, note 36, citing with approval Chief Justice Hughes; Yntema, "The American Law Institute" in *Legal Essays . . . to Orrin McMurray* (1935), 657, 674.

and of Criminal Procedure and the investigation of the federal administrative agencies.

The great difficulties that have attended the preparation of the *Restatement* illustrate pointedly the obstacles that confront us in modernizing the law. Despite its limitations, it will prove of great assistance in the great task of making the law fit the needs of the times. Indeed, its very limitations may serve as a warning against repeating them.

The reworking of our law, moreover, must be based on present economic, political, social conditions, and apparent trends into the future. To the analytical and historical study of the law must be added the sociological approach, and because experiments are not as available in the law as they are in the natural sciences, we must resort to the comparative study of the law. Habitually we resort to comparisons and analogies in deciding cases in the courts, not only utilizing the authorities in our own state but also borrowing freely from the experience of other common-law jurisdictions in our search for sound principles of law adapted to the needs of the time. Legal scholars, however, with rare exceptions have avoided the comparative method of studying law on a grand scale, even though the comparative method comes nearer to the scientific methods of modern research than any other method open to the law.

The reasons for the failure to pursue the comparative method of studying law more assiduously are not hard to find. The difficulties arising from differences in nomenclature in different systems of law and from the necessity of comprehending two or more systems of law in their entirety before undertaking to write about any one phase of them comparatively (for there is no gainsaying the truth that law, like history in Maitland's aphorism, is a "seamless web") are very real. To these must be added the heavy task of understanding the economic, political, and social background of each system of law studied comparatively, for the significance of a system of law cannot be grasped apart from the environment in which it functions. Most important and to the legal scholar most burdensome of all is the need of finding out how the particular subject under consideration actually *works* in each of the legal systems under review, as distinguished from what has been written about it in the books. Thus Justice Brandeis, in emphasizing the need for study of contemporary conditions as the basis for law, illustrated his point by telling how the Montenegro Code was drafted. A learned professor was requested to perform this task.

"Instead of utilizing his great knowledge of laws to draft a code, he proceeded to Montenegro, and for two years literally made his home with the people, studying everywhere their customs, their practices, their needs, their beliefs, their points of view. Then he embodied in law the life the Montenegroes lived. They respected that law; because it expressed the will of the people." [56]

[56] "The Living Law," 10 *Ill. L. Rev.* 461, 471 (1916).

The researcher in comparative law cannot hope to do all of his work in the library or in his study. He must venture forth into the places where the law is in daily operation, and he must not only observe what is going on there, but he must make searching inquiry from men who are expert in dealing with the law in action. Only thus can he hope to avoid the pitfall of finding superficial resemblances or differences in the systems of law under review, when in fact no such resemblances or differences exist.

The greatest deterrent to the comparative study of law from the standpoint of the legal scholar has yet to be mentioned. It is the provincial, one might almost say the parochial, attitude of our bench and bar toward "foreign law," meaning the law of any country other than our own. What a change from the post-Revolutionary attitude of a century and a half ago, when we find the pages of Kent and Story illuminated by numerous references to the great writers on the civil law and when our reports were being enriched by the deliberate use of French authorities! Speaking of his work on the Supreme Court of New York before he became chancellor, Kent said: "The Judges were republicans & very kindly disposed to everything that was French, & this enabled me without exciting any alarm or jealousy to make free use of such [French and civil] authorities & thereby enrich our commercial law." [57] The change in the intellectual attitude of the profession toward

[57] Kent, autobiographical letter in *Select Essays in Anglo American Legal History*, 836–843. (1907).

"foreign" law since post-Revolutionary days is not to our credit.

Enough has been said, I think, to make it clear that the new projects should not take the form of a code. A code looks like a boon until you have to use it. This year we are celebrating the sesquicentennial of the Code Napoléon. It is interesting to note that what corresponds to our law of torts is embraced in five brief sections of that Code, while in our law it takes four stout volumes of the American Law Institute *Restatement of the Law of Torts* to cover the subject. The Code Napoléon does not attempt to cover everything. It deals rather with principles and standards. To meet specific situations the French, like ourselves, must resort to judge-made law. We have likewise seen that casting the *Restatement of the Law* into the form of a code has not improved its usefulness for us. The new work we have been discussing obviously should take the traditional form of a textbook commentary on the law.

The project naturally divides itself into several parts: (1) substantive judge-made law, (2) substantive statutory law, (3) procedural rules, (4) the court structure, *i.e.* the jurisdiction of the courts, (5) administrative procedure, (6) legislative process, (7) principles of judicial administration.

We must recognize as fundamental our need to regain the concept of the law as a system—a scientific, interrelated body of knowledge—and not a mere mass of technical rules, what Holmes years ago called "a ragbag of details." We need, moreover, to treat the law as one of the social sciences, premised on the nature of man as a social animal [58] and the actualities of our social life. This is obviously a necessary requirement, but it carries with it a heavy burden of preliminary study. We need to recognize concretely and at every turn the tradition of our law for giving the individual the greatest possible freedom consistent with the equal rights of others and with the needs of society, and that such freedom necessarily changes in its outward phases from time to time with changes in the social and physical environment of the age. Most important of all, we shall never dare to tackle the task unless we recover the conviction that dominated society a century and a half ago, that individual men have the capacity by study, reason, and consequent action to stake out the course of the future rather than merely to observe social forces, powerless to change them.

No law school solicitous for the future of the law as well as for the training of its students should have to be coaxed into undertaking the functions of a law center. No longer will the law schools be looking exclusively to what the law has been and is, but they will be concerned also with what the law should be and how to bring it about. They will give their thoughts to the living law. In doing so they will breed an inspired corps of students, who will feel that they, too, are being trained to take an active part in the development of the law. The study of the corpus of the law in the law schools

[58] Thorndike, *Human Nature and the Social Order*, 926–956 (1940).

by experts, both professorial and from outside, will develop among the students an enthusiasm for the law as an institution which has not been known since the law schools of Ravenna, Bologna, and Padua began to teach Roman law in the eleventh and twelfth centuries. They will be studying and teaching not merely law as it is found in the books, but law as it is in action. The study of law in action will drive us to an examination of the social, political, and economic forces that are moulding the law. Years ago, Mr. Justice Holmes said: "If your subject is law, the roads are plain to anthropology, the science of man, to political economy, the theory of legislation, ethics, and thus by several paths to your final view of life." [59] It was Holmes, too, who prophesied half a century ago: "The black-letter man may be the man of the present, but the man of the future is the man of statistics and the master of economics." [60]

The fruits of studies of the law centers in the improvement of the law will, of course, be open to all and subject to the criticism of all, from student to practitioner and from legislator to administrator. From the Advisory Committees on Federal Rules of Civil and Criminal Procedure and from judicial conferences of judges and lawyers, we have learned the great value of consultation and free discussion by experts with

[59] Holmes, "The Profession of the Law," in *Collected Legal Papers,* 29, p. 30 (1920).

[60] Holmes, "The Path of the Law," in *Collected Legal Papers* 167, p. 187 (1920).

varied experience. In each state, moreover, there should be the most general cooperation of all of the law schools so that the public may avail itself of all the talent at its disposal.

There is no doubt that the project we are advocating will be an expensive one, but the people of this country have never hesitated to provide the means for achieving justice, nor will they now. And we should consider that the initial cost will in the long run mean a tremendous saving. Although based on a general and even theoretical reexamination of the law, it will serve to decrease the amount of time needed in which to find the law on a given topic. It takes two or three times longer today to uncover the law on a given point than it did twenty-five years ago, due to the increase in the number of decisions, statutes, and of administrative regulations and decisions. Such a revision would serve society by reducing the cost of the law both to litigants and to government.

Thus far, I have been speaking primarily of substantive judgemade law. Let me now turn to substantive statutory law. While a law center can do much to aid our legislatures in long-distance planning, American legislatures are inclined to prefer their own independent agencies, and in this field some of them have made remarkable strides forward. There are three agencies which we will refer to separately: First, legislative councils in some of the states, like Oklahoma and Wisconsin, are doing extraordinary work in uncovering the raw materials of legislation.[61] Second, bill-drafting bureaus are improving the technical draftsmanship of statutes in many of the states. Thirdly, in a few states like New York and Wisconsin continuous statutory revision has been entrusted to specialized agencies with remarkable success.[62] Thus in Wisconsin permanent statute revision at each biennial session of the legislature results in cutting down the size of the statute book by a few pages, despite extensive current legislative activity. These three legislative agencies are distinct, and the best results are to be found when they are performed by separate groups. They require different intellectual and professional qualities, and the time for the performance of their function is different. Only one major difficulty suggests itself in the legislative field: legislatures, not withstanding the fact that they are so largely made up of lawyers, are prone to be much more interested in the solution of economic, governmental, and social problems than they are in overcoming technical defects in the law. Legislatures are jealous of their independence of the other branches of government, and

[61] The legislative council movement is regarded by political scientists generally as perhaps the most significant service agency development in this country, *The Book of the States 1952–53*, p. 115. 29 states now have legislative councils or council-type agencies, Davey, "The Legislative Council Movement 1933–1953," a 1953 special research report for Iowa Economic Studies. See Guild, "Legislative Councils: Objectives and Accomplishments," 22 State Government 217, 226 (Sept. 1949).

[62] See Stone and Pettee, "Revision of Private Law," 54 *Harv. L. Rev.* 221 (1940).

they are much more likely to take kindly to suggestions coming from the impartial researches of law centers than they are from any governmental source outside their own department. Certainly in the solution of problems of legal reform in contrast to social reform the law schools are qualified to give the legislatures the impartial aid they need.

If we take the point of view, as we should, that procedure is merely a means to an end, and that that end is the achievement of justice, it follows not only historically but logically that the function of improving this phase of the law should be committed to the courts, since they are in the best position to deal with it. Dean Pound has analyzed the historical and practical justification for rule-making by the courts [63] and Dean Wigmore has summarized them succinctly:

"1. All rules of procedure in courts, not expressly or impliedly prescribed by the constitution, fall under the judiciary power, for the purpose of making or changing them.

"2. All rules of procedure made by a Supreme Court are valid, notwithstanding any enactment of the legislature that may be inconsistent.

"3. All rules of procedure declared by the legislature are void, and have only such effect as the comity of

[63] Pound, "Procedure Under Rules of Court in New Jersey," 66 *Harv. L. Rev.* 28 (Nov. 1952).

the judiciary may give by following them in the absence of any rule made by the judiciary." [64]

Problems of reforming procedure have been discussed in Chapter III, but even in this field, which is peculiarly one for the members of the profession who habitually work in the courtroom, a law center may be of very real help in supplying comparative data from other states and countries and evaluating such material.

There is, however, one phase of procedure in the broadest sense that the courts and the bar have proved themselves unable to modernize without the aid of laymen generally. At least that has been the experience in England and in New Jersey. What we need everywhere is a simple, flexible organization of courts at the local, county, and state level, with judicial power distributed according to the needs of the times. Likewise the bench and bar have not been able in most instances to agree on the best method of selecting judges. These fundamental phases of court structure and of judicial personnel lie in the field of constitutional revision where the people generally must take the lead with the assistance of such judges and lawyers as are willing to help them. The law centers may at least assist in the assembling of material for the use of constitutional conventions, and in informing the public of the need for change.

[64] Wigmore, "Legislature Has No Power in Procedural Field," 20 *J. Am. Jud. Soc.* 159, p. 160 (1936); see Tolman, "Justice and Her Ministers," 1 *Conn. B. J.* 194 (1927).

The improvement of the procedure of the administrative agencies, both state and federal, also presents a peculiar problem. They are outside the jurisdiction of the traditional courts, although as a matter of fact their work is in large part judicial or at least adjudicatory in nature. They belong to a headless fourth branch of the government.[65] Originally each administration agency had delegated to it by the legislature complete power to

[65] "The Executive Branch of the Government of the United States has . . . grown up without plan or design . . . To look at it now, no one would ever recognize the structure which the founding fathers erected a century and a half ago . . . Commissions have been the result of legislative groping rather than the pursuit of a consistent policy . . . They are in reality miniature independent governments set up to deal with the railroad problem, the banking problem, or the radio problem. They constitute a headless 'fourth branch' of the Government, a haphazard deposit of irresponsible agencies and uncoordinated powers . . . There is a conflict of principle involved in their make-up and functions . . . They are vested with duties of administration . . . and at the same time they are given important judicial work . . . The evils resulting from this confusion of principles are insidious and far-reaching . . . Pressures and influences properly enough directed toward officers responsible for formulating and administering policy constitute an unwholesome atmosphere in which to adjudicate private rights. But the mixed duties of the commissions render escape from these subversive influences impossible. Furthermore, the same men are obliged to serve both as prosecutors and as judges. This not only undermines judicial fairness; it weakens public confidence in that fairness. Commission decisions affecting private rights and conduct lie under the suspicion of being rationalizations of the preliminary findings which the Commission, in the role of prosecutor, presented to itself." *Report of the President's Committee on Administrative Management,* 32–33, 39–40 (1937).

make rules governing its own procedure; oddly enough, the legislative branch perceived no difficulty in confiding to administrative bodies, often made up largely of laymen, the power to regulate procedure, which in many states has been denied to the courts. In these circumstances it naturally followed that there was no uniformity in the procedure of the various administrative agencies. Indeed, in many instances the procedure was never formalized, or at least never publicized. This produced such an administrative chaos that the Federal Administrative Procedure Act [66] became inevitable, and a few states have followed this example by passing similar acts. Such legislation is helpful so far as it goes, but often all too many agencies are exempted, and halfway measures falling far short of traditional procedural safeguards have been adopted. Such has been the influence of the administrative agencies with the legislative branch. The chief defect of administrative procedure acts, however, has been that they do not permit ready amendment when new and better procedures have been developed or are suggested. The remedies for many of these defects may be found in the recently published report of the Hoover Commission Task Force.

The work of improving the procedure of administrative bodies even in their judicial aspect cannot and should not be committed to the courts in view of the doctrine of the separation of powers or on practical grounds. Nor would it be any more feasible to commit it to the chief executive either in state or nation. The

[66] 60 Stat. 237.

best suggestion that has yet been made is to delegate the power to an office of administrative procedure,[67] analogous to the administrative office of the courts. The chief difficulty in creating such an office lies in determining who should appoint its personnel. In the work of an office of administrative procedure, the experts of a law center could be of great assistance.

There is also great need for improving legislative procedure. Of all the departments of government the legislative branch has made the least progress in modernizing and regularizing its methods, despite the need to meet its increasing responsibilities. Congress did make significant progress in the Legislative Reorganization Act of 1946,[68] but the distinguished authors of that act would be the first to admit that it did not go far enough.[69] Here again is a field where the law centers of the country could be of great assistance in studying the problems and coming forward with recommendations for our overworked legislatures.

The finest system of rules and principles of substantive law adapted to the needs of our times, the simplest system of courts, the best judges and the most flexible rules of procedure, will not give litigants what they are entitled to unless they are soundly administered. Broad general rules of administration, like all rules of procedure, must stem from the court of last resort, but the

[67] Schwartz, "Administrative Procedure Act in Operation," 29 *N.Y.U.L. Rev.* 1173, at 1221 (June 1954).

[68] 60 Stat. 812.

[69] Galloway, *Congress at the Crossroads* (1946).

development of the new art and science of judicial administration is the peculiar responsibility of the head of the court of last resort. He should, of course, have the assistance of the presiding judges of all the courts in the state and the constant aid of an administrative office of the courts. But in the last analysis the responsibility must be his, even though the burden imposed thereby is considerable and unremitting. I am convinced that Chief Justice Hughes was right when he said, as he often did, that he regarded his administrative work as of greater significance in the improvement of the administration of justice than he did his opinion writing.

The project for the modernization of the law through the work of law centers has, I submit, the great advantages, first, of paying respect to the doctrine of the separation of powers; second, of avoiding politics and the clash of personalities and the jealousies which so often exist between the different departments of government; and third, of employing those who are best equipped for the task. It is a plan that allows the general consultation of all interested people, and it calls into active play the resources of our law schools which have been too long neglected. The project to which they are being asked to contribute will not be an ivory tower study but will call in experts from active life in the law who are closely in touch with the realities of current legal practice. It will be concerned with the environment of the law, present and prospective. It will employ, among others, the comparative approach, and it will search for universal rules wherever they are to be found.

In a period of crisis and rapid change, such as the one in which we are living, our complacency with the law and its operation cannot but be profoundly shaken. Our first impulse is to try to avoid the tremendous task which is clearly imposed on the legal profession. Reflection, however, will drive us to the necessity for action: first, we must all realize that never in recorded history has there been a civilization that has survived without a system of law adapted to its peculiar needs; second, our own record in recent years is one to give us hope. In the face of political pressures both at home and abroad, the retention and development of our freedom is the supreme concern of our times. The struggle of centuries in England for freedom culminated in the acceptance of the doctrine of the supremacy of law, and that doctrine has been expanded here not only in our written constitutions but in the very spirit of our people. Despite our more than occasional lapses from vigilance in the protection of our rights, our freedom has grown from year to year. The protection of our growing concept of freedom in the rapidly shifting environment of our times and in the face of many adverse forces is the grand task of American law today. Justice between individuals necessarily follows in the wake of freedom of the citizen in relation to his government. Indeed, complete justice is possible only in the realm of freedom, where justice is a matter of right and not merely of governmental grace.

The operation of a law center will inevitably impose

substantial burdens on the law faculties and the men they call to their aid, but it is difficult to see in what other way we can hope to adapt the law to the needs of our changing civilization. I believe that the only way to bring together and harmonize the discordant elements in the law is the same method of patient study followed by courageous action that has been effective in the earlier periods of legal history, and that the best place to do this is in the proposed law centers. Never has our profession faced a greater challenge. Never has the profession in this country been as well organized as it is today. Never have the rewards of courage and far-sightedness promised to be so great. At every point of the law there must be a calm review to achieve the greatest possible individual freedom consistent with the requirements of society as a whole, and a painstaking reform of the law to eliminate outmoded technicalities and to assure the orderly preservation of human rights. Our forefathers solved similar problems, albeit on a lesser scale, but with smaller resources by far than ours. May we have the strength and courage and wisdom to meet the problems of the law in our day with equal courage and zeal.

> *For what avail the plough or sail,*
> *Or law or life, if freedom fail.*

Index

Act of Settlement, 13

administration, courts and their business, in the states, 96; *see also* judicial administration

administration of justice: achievement of improvements, 7-8; importance of, 35; professional opposition to reforms, 4; public irritation at defects, 135

administrative agencies, procedural reforms, 179-180

administrative law: inferior quality of, 140; lack of publication, unknowability, 138-139

Administrative Office of the Courts: need for, 10; New Jersey, organization and functions of, 97-106; United States, 8, 96, 106-121

Advisory Committee on Federal Rules of Civil Procedure, 56

Advisory Committee on Federal Rules of Criminal Procedure, 67

air space, modern problems of, 136

Allegheny County, Pennsylvania, congestion of litigation, 83

American Bar Association: Committee on Uniform Judicial Procedure, 58; Committees on Improving the Administration of Justice, 8; court-packing, plan, defeat of, 21; interest in judicial administration, 8; judicial recall, defeat of, 21; Judicial Section, 108; judicial selection plan, 30-31; minimum standards of judicial administration, program for, 8; research center, 158; Section on Criminal Law, 37

American colonies, judges in, 14

American Judicature Society, *Journal* of, and judicial reform, 7

American Law Institute, 9; Code of Criminal Procedure, 163; cooperative endeavors of, 168; *Restatement of the Law,* 160-168

American Statute Law (Frederic Stimson), 140

Ames, Dean, on need for treatises, 159-160

appellate courts: England, 72; practices in, one-judge opinions, 70-75; procedure, improvements in, 69

Association of the Bar of the City of New York, *Bad Housekeeping; The Administration in the New York Courts,* 130-131

Austin, Charles, 42

Bacon, Henry Selden, on English fears of a Ministry of Justice, 149-150

Bad Housekeeping; The Administration in the New York Courts, 130-131

Banbury v. The Bank of Montreal, 60

bar, *see* legal profession

Bardell v. Pickwick, 49

Bentham, Jeremy, 49

bill-drafting bureaus, 176

Birkenhead, Lord, and law reform, 148

Blackstone, William, on procedure, 40

Bleak House (Charles Dickens), 48, 84

Bogert, George G., trusts, 158

Boston, congestion of litigation, 82

Brandeis, Justice Louis D., on need to study contemporary conditions as basis for law, 170

Calamandrei, Piero, on position of the continental judge, 151-153

California: courts, administrative machinery, 97; court structure, 39; judges, campaign expenses, 23; judicial selection plan, 30

Canons of Judicial Ethics, 22, 23-25, 27

Cardozo, Justice Benjamin, advocacy of Ministry of Justice, 154

casebooks, concentration on, 160

chancery: Dickens on, 49; jurisdiction, 38; New Jersey, delays in, 83; procedure, practice and remedies, 46-48; U.S., dislike of, 51

Chandler, Henry P., Director, Administrative Office of the United States Court, 116

Chase, Justice Samuel, impeachment of, 21

Chitty, Joseph, *Pleading,* 40

citizens, apathy of, 3

Clark, Chief Judge Charles E., 56; on *Restatement,* 167

Code of Civil Procedure, New York, 50, 54

Code of Criminal Procedure, American Law Institute, 163

Code of Federal Regulations, vast size of, 138

Code of Hammurabi, 161

Code of Justinian, 161

Code of Napoleon, 161, 172

codification, 172

Coke, Sir Edward: and adaptation of law, 141; *Fourth Institute,* 37; on right to air space, 136; on royal prerogative, 13

Coleridge, Lord Chief Justice: on evidence, 45; on special pleading, 41

Colorado, courts, administrative machinery, 97

commercialism and lawyers' opposition to reform, 5

common law: attacks on in U.S., 51; capacity for growth, 137; John Hazard on, 144

Common Pleas, Court of, 38

comparative law, importance and difficulties of study of, 74-75, 169-171

complaint, sufficiency of, 60

Conformity Act, 55

congestion of litigation, 81-85, 95, 114, 132

Connecticut: courts, administrative machinery, 97; Hartford County, congestion of litigation, 83

Cook, Walter Wheeler, criticism of *Restatement,* 167

Cook County, Illinois, congestion of litigation, 82

Corbin, Arthur L., *Contracts,* 158

costs, English problem of, 50-51

courts: administrative machinery for, 89, 96-97; administrative offices of, 10, 97-121; attacks on, 20-21; bipartisan, 33; common law, 37-38; congestion of, 81-85, 95, 114, 132; delays in, 76-78; Dickens on, 49; England, reorganization of, 50; federal, *see* federal courts; improvements in, 36; jurisdiction, 39, 44; in New Jersey, *see* New Jersey; in New York, *see* New York; organization, requirements of adequate, 39, 86; personnel, 11; procedural rules and reforms, 57, 90, 177-178; simplified system necessary, 86

crime, in United States, 3

criminal procedure, reform of, Federal Rules, 67

criminal trials, expedition of, 96

Cummings, Atty. Gen. Homer S., 55, 111

Daniell, Edmund R., *Equity Pleading and Practice*, 40

Declaration of Independence, 14

Delaware: bipartisan judiciary, 33; courts, simplified structure, 39; judicial reform, 9

Democratic Review, on delays in N.Y. courts, 82

Dickens, Charles: *Bleak House*, 48, 84; *Pickwick Papers*, 49

discovery, modern rules for, 59, 91, 95

Eldon, Lord Chancellor, 84

England: appellate practice, 72; barristers' skill in conduct of trial, 94; common law procedure, 51; costs, modern problems of, 50; court rules, 50; court system, ancient, complexity of, 37; courts, modern reorganization, 39, 50, 178; develop-
ment of independent judiciary, 12-14; Evershed Committee, 50; evidence, rules, 45-46; Fields' influence on, 54; judges, popular confidence in, 51; judicial reforms, effectiveness of, 9, 50; Judicature Acts, 38, 46, 50, 95-96; jury, use of, 94; Legal Aid Scheme, 50; legal profession, division of, 50; Ministry of Justice, 146; pleadings, sufficiency of, 60-62; procedural reform, 40, 46, 50; selection of judges, 13, 28

equity: procedure, 40; remedies, 46; *see also* chancery

Erle, Sir William, 43

Evershed Committee, Report, 50

evidence: Model Code of, 9; reforms in, 44-46; trial judge, summary of, 53; Uniform Rules of, 9, 46, 74, 163

Exchequer, Court of, 38, 42

fair trial, 68-69

federal administrative decisions and regulations, 138

Federal Administrative Procedure Act, 180

federal courts: abolition of distinction between law and equity, 56; administration of, developments towards effective, 106-121; Administrative Office for, *see* Administrative Office of the United States Courts; assignment of judges, 118-119; congestion in, 114, 116-120; executive head, lack of, 117; Fourth Circuit, annual conference, 115; immense business of, 107; judges: insufficient number of, 117; judicial conferences

federal courts (*continued*)
and councils, 113-114; organization of, 39, 107; pretrial conference, use of, 120-121; Senior Circuit Judges, Annual Conference, 108-114

Federal Regulations, Code of, 138

Federal Rules of Civil Procedure, 8, 55-60, 95; Rules 1 and 2, 58

Federal Rules of Criminal Procedure, 8, 67-68

fictions, use of, 46

Field Code, 50, 54

Field, David Dudley, 146; on delays in justice, 81; procedural reform leadership, 53-54

Fourth Circuit, annual conferences, 115

Fourth Institute (Coke), 37

France: Jeffersonian admiration of civil law, 51; Kent's use of French jurists, 143, 171; Ministry of Justice in, 149

Gallup poll, on judges, 25

Georgia, judges, selection and tenure, 14-15

Giles, Senator, critical of courts, 20

Goodhart, Sir Arthur L., 148

Gower, L. C. B., on costs, 50

Graigola Merthyr Ltd. v. Swansea Corp., 51

Haldane, Lord Chancellor, 146

Hammurabi, Code of, 161

Hartford County, Connecticut, congestion of litigation, 83

Hazard, John, on the common law, 144

Herbert, A. P., *Matrimonial Causes Act,* 147

Hewart, Lord Chief Justice, 148

Holdsworth, William, 48, 145; *History of English Law,* 37

Holmes, Justice Oliver W.: on law and other studies, 174; on technical rules, 172

Holtzoff, Judge Alexander, on assignment of federal judges, 118

Hughes, Chief Justice Charles E.: 113, 140, 182; on Administrative Office Act, 112; on goals of *Restatement,* 165

Illinois, Cook County, congestion of litigation, 82

impeachment of judges, 20-21

Indiana, elected judiciary, 15

Institute of Judicial Administration, statistics on courts congestion, 81

Iowa, courts, administrative machinery, 97

Jackson, Atty. Gen. Robert H., 67

Jackson, President Andrew, on tenure of public officials, 19

Jacksonian Revolution, effect on bar, courts and judiciary, 17-22, 142

Jarndyce and Jarndyce, 48, 84

Jefferson, President Thomas, 17, 20

Jeffersonian, attacks on common law, 51

Jenk's *Digest of English Civil Law,* 162

Journal of the American Judicature Society, 7

Jowitt, Lord Chancellor, 28

judges: ad interim appointments, effects of, 21-22; American Bar Association plan for selection of, 30; appointive system, 32;

assignment of, 87-88, 98, 102; bipartisan system, value of, 33; California plan, 30; campaigns for office, 19, 22; civil law, position of, 151-154; common law, powers of, 51-52; division of work among, 89; elective system, problems of, and politics, 15-19, 21-22, 26, 31-32; England, popular confidence in, 51; Gallup poll on, 25; great, epitomized the law, 145-146; honesty of, 25-26; impeachment of, 20-21; improvement in caliber of, 10; individual differences of, 87, 89; independence and impartiality of, 12-17, 20; lawyers' responsibility in selection, 29; limitations on trial, in U.S., 52-53; Missouri plan, 30; opposition of, to procedural changes, danger of, 4; politics and, 22-25, 28; pretrial conference, tasks of, 64-66; qualifications of, 11-12, 27; recall of, 21; reform of the law by, 146; reports to administrative director of the courts, 90; securing prompt decisions from, 80; selection of, England, 13, 28; selection of, U.S., 14-17, 28-32; Soviet Russia, elected, 17; standards for, needed, 27; tasks, variety of, 87; tenure in U.S., 14-17, 19; trial without a jury, 46; work reports, 89, 102

Judicature Acts, England, 38, 50, 95-96

judicial administration: American Bar Association, interest in reforms, 8; court made rules for, 181; federal courts, 106-121; in the states, 96; need for adminis- trative machinery and rules, 80, 84, 92, 96-98; New Jersey, 97-105; New York, 121-130; reforms, 7, 8, 181-182

Judicial Conferences: New Jersey, 57, 105; Senior Circuit Judges, 108-114

judicial decisions, great numbers of, still increasing, 137

judicial reform, 7, 9, 132; see also law reform

judicial structure, simplification of, 10

Judiciary Act of 1789, 107

jurisdiction, 39, 44

jury: charge by judge to, 53; examination of, 94; importance of, 11; improvement of, 10; qualifications of, 12; selection, 33-34; significance of, 33; waiver of, 94-95

justice, importance of interest in, 3

Justinian, Code of, 161

juvenile courts and juvenile delinquency, New Jersey, 96

Kefauver Committee, 3

Kent, Chancellor James, and civil law authorities, 143, 171

Kentucky, courts, administrative machinery, 97

Kings County, New York, congestion of litigation, 81

Langdell, Lord, Master of the Rolls, 146

law: and social science, 173; as a system, 172; in action, study of, 173-174; reform of, *see* law reform, respect for, important to survival of popular government, 5 law centers: administrative agencies, procedural reforms, assistance in, 181; and law reform, 156, 176-177; court organization reform, assistance in 178; law schools as, 156, 173; legislative proceduer, assistance in reform of, 181; modernization of law, help in, 182-184; procedural reform, supplying data, 178; study of law in action, 173-174

law's delays: 76-80; elimination of, 10, 80, 92-95, 132-133

law reform: 7-10, 74, 134, 145, 146, 169, 172; England, 147-148; judicial administration, court responsibility for, 181-182; law schools as law centers, leaders in, 155, 182; modernization of substantive law, 10, 135-136, 141, 156, 158, 169, 182; laymen's role in, 38, 85-86, 156-157, 178; professional opposition to, dangers of, 4; project for, outlined, 172-181; task of legal profession and public, 134-135, 183-184; U.S. and Ministry of Justice, 154

law schools: as centers for reform, 156-158, 173; faculties as leaders of reform, 155; teaching of procedure, 132

Laws, Chief Judge Bolitha J., pretrial conference demonstration, 66

lawyers, see legal profession

laymen, court organization reform, participation in, 38, 85-86, 156-157, 178

Legal Aid, England, 50

legal education: shortcomings of, in United States, 154-155; see also law schools

legal profession: adaptation of the law, its task, 141-144; challenge to, of law reform, 183-184; commercialism as cause of opposition to reform, 7; England, division of, 50; failure to lead, in Jacksonian era, 142; importance of, to the courts, 11; increasing interest in reform, 7; public law, neglect of, 5; responsibilities of, 28-29, 35, 144

legislation, vast bulk of, 138

legislative councils, Oklahoma and Wisconsin, 175

legislative procedure, reforms needed, 181

Legislative Reorganization Act of 1946, 181

legislature: agencies assisting, 175-176; law centers, as sources of suggestions to, 177

Lewis, Dr. William Draper, on Restatement, 164-165, 166

litigants, dissatisfaction with court procedure, 4

litigation, elimination of chronic congestion, 81-84

Livingston, Edward, 146

Louisiana, courts, administrative machinery, 97

Lummus, Justice, on judges and politics, 28

Madison, James, preparation for Constitutional Convention, 143

Magna Carta, 12

Maitland, F. W., 142

Mansfield, Lord, adaptation of the law by, 143; attempt to merge law and equity, 38

Marbury v. Madison, Jefferson's criticism of, 20

Marshall, Chief Justice John, 16, 20

Maryland, courts, administrative machinery, 97

Massachusetts: delays in courts, 82; judicial appointments, 32

Michigan: courts, administrative machinery, 97; elected judiciary, 15

minimum standards for judicial administration, American Bar Association program for, 8

Ministry of Justice, 146-150

Mississippi, elected judiciary, 15

Missouri: courts, administrative machinery, 97; judicial selection plan, 30

Mitchell, Atty. Gen. William D., 55

Model Code of Evidence, American Law Institute, 9, 163

Napoleon, Code, 161, 172

National Conference of Commissioners on Uniform State Laws, Uniform Rules of Evidence, 9, 46, 74, 163

New Jersey: administrative measures expediting court work, 98-99; Administrative Office of the Courts, 97-106; appellate court practices, 72; assignment of judges, 102; bipartisan judiciary, 33; chancery, delays in, 83-84; Chief Justice, administrative head of the courts, 98; congested calendars, elimination of, 76-77, 83-85, 93; courts, extent of business, 101; courts, numbers of prior to 1947, 38; courts,

simplified organization, 39, 86; county courts, retention, 86; criminal calendar, control of, 96; judges' work reports, 102; judicial appointments, 32; judicial conferences, 57-58; juvenile courts, 96; lay participation in court reform, 9, 178; pretrial conference, mandatory, 63-65; procedural reform, 58-59; rule making, 57; special pleading in, 43-44; statistics, collection of, 101; Superior Court, 86, 98; Supreme Court, 97, 101

New York: Association of the Bar of the City of, 130-131; Code of Civil Procedure, 50, 54, 126; county, congestion of litigation, 81; "court administration" act, analysis of defects of, 121-131; courts, improvement in, judicial leadership, 132; elected judiciary, 15; statutory revision, continuous, 176; Temporary Commission on Courts, 121

North Carolina, courts, administrative machinery, 97

office of administrative procedure, 180-181

Oklahoma, legislative council, 175

Oregon, administrative machinery, 97

Otis, Judge Merrill E., on common law powers of the judge, 52

Panama Refining Co. v. Ryan, 140

Parke, Baron, 41-44

Parker, Chief Judge John J.: Fourth Circuit Conference, 115; on federal court administrative system, 107, 111

Parker, Lord, on pleading, 60

Peck, Presiding Justice David W., relief of congested calendars, 132

Pennsylvania, political activities of judges, 22

personnel, precedence of problems of, 7

Pickwick Papers (Charles Dickens), 49

Pittsburgh, Pennsylvania, congestion of litigation, 83

pleadings: amendment, liberal, 62; function under modern rules, 60-62; special, subtleties of, 41

Plowden, Francis P., 37

politics, and judges, *see* judges

Pound, Roscoe: advocacy of Ministry of Justice, 154; on David Dudley Field, 53; on rule making by the courts, 177; "The Causes of Popular Dissatisfaction with the Administration of Justice," 6; writings of, 159-160

pretrial conference: casualty companies, participation in, 66; federal courts, use of, 121; procedure at, 64; rules for, utility of, 59, 63-66

pretrial procedures: discovery, availability under modern rules, 59, 91, 95

procedure: appellate, 69; changes in, summary, 74; common law rules of service, 41; comparative study of, importance, 36, 74; court-made rules, 90-91, 177; English, 44; Federal Rules of Civil Procedure, 55, 58; Field Code, 53-54; judicial opposition to changes in, 4; law school

teaching of, 133; lawyers' opposition to reform, 4; legislative control of, 44; modern reforms, acceptance and effect of, 36-37, 55, 58, 74, 177; precedence of problems of, 7; special pleading, 41-43; trial, 45

Progressive Party, attack on courts, 21

public, and improvement of judicial system, 134; *see* laymen

Puerto Rico courts: administrative machinery, 97; simplified structure of, 39

Queen's Bench, Court of, 38

Queens County, New York, congestion of litigation, 81

recall of judges, 21

referees, restriction of use of, 92-93

Restatement of the Law, American Law Institute: aims of, 164, 165; code form, 161; criticism of its limitations, 161-167; utility of, 168

Rhode Island: courts, administrative machinery, 97; judicial tenure, 14

Roosevelt, President Franklin D., court packing plan, 21

Roosevelt, President Theodore, attack on courts, 21

rotation in office, 19

rule making: courts, continuity of process of, 57, 90; methods of, 56; U.S. Supreme Court, 55; *see also* procedure

Schuster, Lord, 148, on police state, 150

Scott, Austin W., *Trusts,* 158

senior circuit judges, Annual Judicial Conference of, 108-114; disapproval of "confidential briefs," 68

Shelley's Case, 148

Shelton, Thomas W., 55

Smith, F. E., *see* Birkenhead, Lord

Soviet Russia, elected judiciary, 17

special pleading, 41

statistics, collection of, 181-182

statute law, inferior quality of, 140

Statute of Westminster II, 46

statutory revision, 176

Stern, Chief Justice, on jury waiver, 95

Stimson, Frederic, *American Statute Law,* 140

Stone, Chief Justice, on commercialism and the legal profession, 5

Story, Mr. Justice, 3, 171

substantive law: adaptation in early United States, 51; adjustment to contemporary needs, 6, 10, 136, 141-142, 156, 169; growth of, vast bulk, 137-140; inconsistencies of, 141; judge made, reform in law centers, 173-174; modernization, necessary and difficult, 135, 156, 169; professional adaptation to new needs in other critical periods, 141; reform, need of, 135; statutory, 175-176

Suffolk County, Massachusetts (Boston), congestion of litigation, 82

Taft, Chief Justice: on commercialism and the legal profession, 5; on Judicial Conference of Senior Circuit Judges, 108-109

textbooks, influence of, and need for modern, 158-160

Thayer, James B., 46

Third Circuit, Judicial Council, activities of, 113

Tidd's *Practice,* 40

trial: evidence at, limitations upon, 44; procedure, 45, 51; without jury, 46

Uniform Rules of Criminal Procedure, 163

Uniform Rules of Evidence, 9, 46, 74, 163

United States: Administrative Office of the Courts, 8, 96, 106 121; Advisory Committees on Federal Rules, 55-56, 67; chancery, dislike of, 51; courts, *see* federal courts; English common law procedure in, 51; judges: early limits on authority of, 52; Judicial Conference of Senior Circuit Judges, 68-69, 108-114; post-revolutionary problems of, 51; procedural reform, 51-53; rule making power, 55; substantive law, *see* substantive law; trial procedure in, 51-53

Virginia, courts, administrative machinery, 97

Walsh, Senator Thomas A., 55

Webster, Daniel, on importance of justice, 3

Wesley, Reverend John, on chancery bill, 47

Westbury, Lord Chancellor, 146

Westminster II, Statute of, 46

Wigmore, John H., 6, 46, 79, 158; on rule making by the court, 177
Willer, Sir James, 42
Williston, Samuel, 158

Wisconsin: legislative council, 175; statutory revision, 176
Worcester County, Mass., congestion of litigation, 82
writs, 41, 44

DATE DUE